A FEAST *of* SERENDIB

RECIPES FROM SRI LANKA

Illustrations by Pamudu Tennakoon
Book design by Jeremy John Parker

Photo Credits: Front cover and pages 52, 111, 124, 132, 160, 164, 167, 174, 190, 192, 202, 205, 225 and 268 by Paul Goyette; photo on page 94 by Suchetha Wijenayake; all other photos (except for the one of Pamudu Tennakoon) by Mary Anne Mohanraj, or from her family's archives.

WWW.MARYANNEMOHANRAJ.COM
WWW.SERENDIBKITCHEN.COM
WWW.SERENDIBPRESS.COM

For more information, please contact:
Mascot Books
620 Herndon Parkway, Suite 320
Herndon, VA 20170
info@mascotbooks.com

CPSIA Code: PRTWP0919A
ISBN-13: 978-1-64543-275-3

Printed in Malaysia

For my children–
    Kaviarasi Ann Jacintha
    Anandan Mohan McLeod
       –that they may remember

Mary Anne Mohanraj

A FEAST *of* SERENDIB

RECIPES FROM SRI LANKA

Illustrations by Pamudu Tennakoon

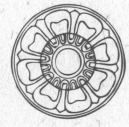

MASCOT BOOKS

CONTENTS

APPETIZERS / 'SHORT EATS' *and* SNACKS

EGGS, POULTRY, *and* MEAT

FISH *and* SEAFOOD

VEGETABLES

ACCOMPANIMENTS

GRAINS

DRINKS

SWEETS

INTRODUCTION

The first time I started writing a Sri Lankan cookbook, *A Taste of Serendib,* it was meant to simply be a Christmas present for my mother—writing down some of her recipes. The book offered a few recipes in each section, and featured sketches that a friend drew, illustrating me and my mother cooking, including a few choice quotes of my mother scolding me in the kitchen: "You cannot read and stir at the same time!"

It quickly spiraled into a book, but the focus was still simple—what little I knew of her recipes. It was designed to be accessible to college students, like the one I was at the time. I was an immigrant who had come to America very young, had grown up eating rice and curry every night, but had only a tenuous connection to the food culture of the homeland.

My mother had had to make many adaptations when she came to America in 1973. She used ketchup instead of tomatoes, for example, because she didn't have access to coconut milk, and cow's milk didn't have sufficient sweetness. (Ketchup also sped along the sauce-making process, since it's basically a cooked down mixture of tomatoes, vinegar, sugar, and salt.) My mother's recipes had already changed in America, and as I made them myself, they changed further, adapting to my tastes. When I gave my mother the finished book, she was pleased, but also immediately started pointing out where I'd gotten things wrong. I threatened to do a second edition of the book, with "Amma's corrections" all through it in red. I still think that would have been a good book, but she didn't go for it.

1

So the book stayed as it was for many years. It could have been left there. But instead, more than a decade later, I started working on a new cookbook, *A Feast of Serendib*.

My husband, Kevin, and I were talking recently about how I choose which projects to work on. There's often a pressure to spend my time and energy on more commercial projects, the ones that have the best odds of a good payout. This new cookbook should sell some copies; hopefully, it'll sell lots of copies. But it's hardly the most commercial project I could work on, and making the recipes, some of them over and over again, trying to get them right, has been exceedingly time-consuming. If it were just about the money, this cookbook would make no sense at all.

But it's rarely just about the money. Over the years since I did the first cookbook, I have added more and more Sri Lankan recipes to my repertoire. My cookbook shelf has been overtaken by Sri Lankan cookbooks: from classics like the *Ceylon Daily News Cookbook*; to conflict-related books like the beautiful and heartbreaking *Handmade*; to fancy coffee table books full of glorious photos like *The Food of Sri Lanka*; to what is still my favorite, Charmaine Solomon's *Complete Asian Cookbook*—her Sri Lankan recipes taste like my mother's, like home.

I enjoy cooking dishes from other cuisines. Ethiopian is one of my favorites, and there are days when I crave sushi. Pizza is a family standby, and my children are built in large part out of mac-and-cheese. But I come back to Sri Lankan food—I cook it at least once or twice, most weeks. These days, I go online and read a dozen different recipes for a dish before I even start making it. I interrogate my Sri Lankan friends (both diasporan and homelander) about their recipes. I want to know how these dishes were typically made, in the villages, for generations and generations back. What should the balance of upu-puli (salty-sour) be? How thick do we want the finished gravy?

If I can't get a certain leafy green considered key to traditional cookery, I feel such frustration. But I try to accept the truth, that I will likely never cook exactly how homeland Sri Lankans would. My adaptations of my mother's adaptations are still tasty.

My husband is white American, for enough generations that he's not sure exactly where all his ancestors came from. Once, when Kevin and I were talking about naming our first child, about whether to give her a Tamil name, he asked whether we wouldn't be better off if we didn't cling so hard to ethnic, racial, nationalist traditions. Divisions. In some ways, I think he's right. Sri Lanka was riven by ethnic conflict for decades, and the country and its people are still dealing with the aftermath—it would be worth giving up much, if you could thereby make the conflicts end.

But this is who we are; this is what it is to be human. We are composed of our mother's hand with a salt shaker, the squeeze of fresh lime at the end of the dish. For those of us who are attenuated from the food of our grandparents and great-grandparents, learning how to cook this food, in its many iterations, can feel like filling a hole in your heart. We named our daughter Kaviarasi in the end, a very old Tamil name, which means 'queen of poetry.' Diasporic friends of my parents sent us thank you notes, for giving her such a classic Tamil name, for keeping the traditions alive.

I choose this. I choose to put time and energy into learning this food, into serving it to my mixed-race children, with the hopes that they will grow to love it too. Kavi comes into the kitchen to ask excitedly, "Oh, are you making the yellow chicken?" That's the Sri Lankan ginger-garlic chicken that she likes better than any other chicken, and when she asks for it, my heart skips a beat.

We come together with other Sri Lankans—homelander and diaspora, Sinhalese and Tamil, Buddhist and Hindu and Christian and Muslim—over delicious shared meals. Sri Lanka has been a multi-ethnic society for over two thousand years, with neighbors of different ethnicities, languages, religions, living side by side. We try to teach our children to be welcoming to all, to share our unique cultural traditions. That is part of what it means to be Sri Lankan, what it has always meant.

Can we choose the good parts of our culture to cherish, and leave the darker aspects behind? I hope so. I hope food can help provide a pathway there. Come together at our table, sharing milk rice and pol sambol, paruppu and crab curry. Linger over the chai—just one more cup. Eat, drink, and share joy.

As for me, I make no claim to authenticity—there are many more authentic Sri Lankan cookbooks, painstakingly researched. But if there was a thin line drawn with that first cookbook, connecting me to the food of my ancestors, then the last few years of researching and adding recipe after recipe to this cookbook have thickened and strengthened the thread of connection, into a sturdy rope. One that you might use when lost, to find your way home.

I've come to appreciate the long history, the gathered wisdom of a thousand thousand cooks, who have known that with the perfection of hoppers at breakfast, all you need is a little fresh coconut sambol to accompany it, with perhaps an egg cracked into the center to steam. The more I cook these recipes, the more I grow to love this food.

I hope other readers of this cookbook will feel the same, and will love Sri Lanka, its food, and most of all, its people, along with me.

—*Mary Anne Amirthi Mohanraj*
August 2019

ETHNIC HERITAGE *and* COLONIAL INFLUENCES

My family is of the Tamil ethnic / cultural / language group, and almost all of the recipes that follow are Sri Lankan Tamil. (I have given Tamil names for some dishes, although for many, using English naming is common—my parents and their siblings will refer to fish cutlets and chicken patties, for example.) About sixteen percent of the Sri Lankan population is Tamil, a large percentage of whom came to Sri Lanka over two thousand years ago, settling primarily in the North and East; our cooking has diverged significantly from that of Indian Tamils from the southernmost state of Tamil Nadu.

My paternal grandfather, C.V.E. Navaratnasingam, principal of Delft Maha Vidyalaya

Another group, the Hill Country / Indian Tamils, were brought over in the 19th and 20th centuries to work the coffee and tea plantations by the colonizers; some also came on their own as merchants and traders. The majority of the island's population is Sinhalese (about seventy-four percent), with a significant population of Moors (speaking Arabic-influenced Tamil, though many are also fluent in Sinhalese). There are also some smaller groups, including Malays and the indigenous Veddahs.

Sri Lanka experienced three waves of colonization—Portuguese (arriving 1505), Dutch (arriving 1602), and British (arriving 1802). All of the colonizing groups, along with the Hakka and Cantonese laborers they brought to Sri Lanka and more recent Chinese migrants, have left their culinary imprint on the island.

SRI LANKAN MEALS

I'm often asked what is characteristic of Sri Lankan food, and how it differs from Indian food. The second question is difficult, because it's usually Americans asking me, and they're used to Americanized Indian food, which is often fairly generic and watered down—not actual food from India, which is dramatically different, depending on whether you're talking Mughal-influenced North Indian cuisine, mostly-vegetarian Gujarati, etc.

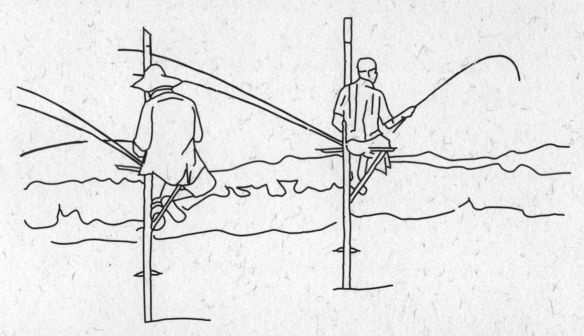

Two main elements of Sri Lankan cuisine are our use of dark-roasted curry powder across the island and goraka (a souring fruit, similar to tamarind) in Sinhalese cooking. You won't find goraka in recipes here, though, as my Tamil family doesn't use it. Other characteristic elements include wholesome red rice, plenty of chili heat, curry leaves, lots of coconut milk and shredded coconut, a bit of pungent dried Maldive fish in many dishes, and usually a touch of tang (from tomato, vinegar, tamarind, or lime). We also eat a wide variety of fish, poultry, and meat dishes, which I think is somewhat unusual in South Asia, given religious prohibitions, but can be traced to a long-standing multiethnic and multi-religious population. An island at the nexus of trade routes absorbs many culinary influences.

Sri Lankan cuisine has particularly strong similarities to Goan cuisine, in the Portuguese influence—more pork and beef than you might find in India generally, more vinegar in the curries, plenty of coconut milk, coconut, and fish, because Goa, like Sri Lanka, is coastal. We tend to not make creamy milk-based curries, the sort you'd find in North India. Sri Lankan cuisine also has commonalities with South Indian cuisine—the dry spiced poriyals, the commonality of sambar and rasam (with plenty of tamarind), with idli, thosai, and uppuma for grain-based dishes.

My mother, Jacintha Mohanraj, my sister, Mirnalini Mohanraj, and my paternal grandmother, Regina Navaratnasingam

I came to America when I was two years old, and so I never ate like a Sri Lankan would back home; for example, I had usually cereal for breakfast growing up in Connecticut. A typical Sri Lankan breakfast is some idli and sambar, or string hoppers and sothi, perhaps with paruppu (lentils). I grew up disliking lentils and have only recently learned to love them, but most people in Sri Lanka eat lots of lentils regularly. If you were feeling fancier, you might make hoppers for breakfast (but you'd have to plan that the night before). Uppuma is also a nice change, usually with some fish curry. I've gotten addicted to eating American pancakes with curry—the sweetness of the pancakes works really well with a spicy curry.

As a child, I would have often eaten a bologna sandwich for lunch, but in Sri Lanka, lunches are rice and curries, often eaten around 3 p.m., and dinners are the same, often eaten around 9 p.m. Generally we would serve plain white rice, a meat curry, and a vegetable curry. Appetizers and fancier accompaniments are usually saved for when guests or more family come over, although you'd likely keep containers of sambol or pickle around, for added flavor. Some of my American friends are surprised when I tell them that I had rice and curry for dinner every single night when I was growing up—what can I say? If your mother is an excellent cook, then you never get bored by a little repetition.

The fancier dishes, the hoppers and pittu and stringhoppers, the patties and cutlets, the milk toffees and rich cake—those were all saved for parties. Usually, we stuffed ourselves on the delectable appetizers (called short eats), but somehow always managed to find room for dinner and then dessert. If you need one more little bite to fill out a table, some fresh fruit sprinkled with cayenne, salt, and lime is always appropriate as appetizer or accompaniment.

Note: Sri Lankans eat with their right hand, not with utensils, generally. It takes a little practice to learn how to make a neat little ball of rice and curry with your fingers, but more than a few of my friends have learned how over the years. Note that many of our recipes use whole spices such as cardamom pods, cloves, and cinnamon, that are not meant to be bitten into—when you're eating with your hands, it's easy to pick out and avoid those as you have dinner.

If you're planning on eating with a fork, you may want to either grind those spices before adding them, use pre-ground versions (generally not as strongly-flavored, so you may want a bit more), or tie them into a bit of cheesecloth that you can fish out before serving (this works better for a more liquid curry). If hosting a dinner party where guests will be eating with their hands, set a finger bowl at each place, so they can rinse and dry their fingers without leaving the table.

A FEW CAVEATS

I learned to cook from watching my mother; I would ask her how to make a dish, and she would say, "Just watch." So I did, and I wrote things down, and sometimes I would pester her with questions: when she tossed in some black mustard seed, I'd ask her how much she'd put in, and when she answered "three pinches", I'd estimate what that meant in teaspoons. I've tried to convert to standard measurements when I can, for your convenience (and if you need metric, I recommend using an online metric converter—if you tell it three cups, it'll tell you how many grams).

My maternal grandmother, mother, and many siblings and other relatives

But I wouldn't recommend being too tied to the precise measurements in the recipes. Learning from my mother, I quickly found that it wasn't much use, trying to write down exact recipes. When I started cooking myself, I found that the appropriate amounts often varied from day to day, depending on a strange chemistry of interactions that I am not skilled enough to describe. Don't be afraid to add a little less cayenne, or a little more milk or ketchup, or vice versa!

Homesick

The problem with going deep
is that you can fall in.

You find yourself reheating
frozen food, a pale imitation
of the real thing. Making
other dishes over and over
trying to remember
decades-old cinnamon
in the nose, lime on the tongue,
chili heat lingering on your lips—
a pain that you seek out repeatedly.

Sometimes you think your heart
can't take it; it would be easier
to order pizza instead. Who
doesn't love melted cheese?

Yet here you are, microwaving
frozen hoppers that you keep
stashed in the basement
deep freeze. Hoarded for
those days when you need
them, even if it hurts.

AGAR-AGAR is a powder, much like plain gelatin. You can often find it at a large organic gourmet store, like Whole Foods, or possibly at your local Indian grocery store.

If you can't find BLACK (OR BROWN) MUSTARD SEED, regular mustard seed will do.

CARDAMOM PODS are available green, white, or black—you want the green cardamom pods (the ones commonly found in American grocery stores) for Sri Lankan cuisine. We generally use them whole in curries, though do be careful not to bite into them when you eat, as they can be unpleasant; if you're worried, you can always tie whole spices into a bit of cheesecloth and let that simmer in a curry sauce, removing before serving. You can also toast the pods, let them cool, and then crack them open and just use the seeds, though that's quite labor intensive. Ground cardamom powder is less flavorful; it loses flavor quickly on grinding.

Buy your CAYENNE at the Indian grocery store if you can—it should be a dark red, and is usually much hotter than American grocery store cayenne. (It may even be labeled in varieties, such as Hot or Extra Hot). If you can't get to such a store, or order it online, use crushed dried red chili pods—Mexican cayenne (a mix of several spices) is not a good substitute. Generally, you'll want to fry the cayenne for a few seconds in

a little hot oil, before adding curry powder or other spices, or it will taste raw in the finished dish. If you start to cough, that's a warning that the cayenne is about to burn. Some recipes will also call for DRIED RED CHILIES, with similar flavor and heat, but different consistency.

TRUE CEYLON CINNAMON is grown in Sri Lanka, and is generally considered higher quality than the cassia cinnamon (hard, tight sticks, difficult to grind) that is much more commonly available. But you can certainly use either in these dishes.

An essential spice for Sri Lankan cooking are CLOVES—use these aromatic flower buds whole in most curries, or powdered in desserts.

CORIANDER SEED is one of the oldest known spices in the world, very aromatic with citrus notes. Dry roast it to release additional flavor, until it turns golden-brown and starts 'popping' in the pan.

Many of my dishes start with sautéing CUMIN SEEDS in oil with onions; cumin has a strong fragrance and lends an essential smoky note to the dishes. If you toast it, be careful to stir on low heat—cumin burns very easily, and would then be quite bitter in your dish.

CURRY LEAVES are broad, level, dark-green leaves, thumb-sized or larger, which can be found in a good Indian grocery store, either fresh, frozen, or dried, and which are becoming more available in regular American grocery stores. There is no good substitute—if you can't find them, leave them out of the recipe. The thin, rounded silvery leaves of the *curry plant* you can occasionally find at garden stores are not meant for cooking—they merely smell curry-like. You can now buy curry leaves online, through Amazon and elsewhere.  If they arrive fresh and it's more than you can use, freeze the extra (you can just add them frozen to a curry, without thawing first). If they arrive dried, they won't be quite as strong, so use a bit more. My recipes generally call for a dozen curry leaves; this is an estimate, and a few more or less won't matter.

Sri Lankan cooking is often hotter than Indian; if you're not used to it, trying making the recipe with only half the roasted CURRY POWDER and/or cayenne the first time around. Indian curry powder is not a good substitute for Sri Lankan; look for Sri Lankan or Jaffna roasted curry powder online or in stores for these recipes, or make your own, following the recipe provided. This is *key* to getting the flavors right.

Never buy your SHREDDED COCONUT in the baking aisle—it's almost certainly sweetened. Try the Indian grocery or the bulk foods section of your local grocery store instead. If you can find frozen shredded coconut, even better; it will have a fresher taste. Or, if you want, you can buy whole coconut and a coconut grater to (laboriously) grate your own, as my mother did.

Another essential spice is FENNEL SEED, offering a sweet, grassy flavor with notes of anise and licorice. It's supposedly good for your digestion, and candy-coated fennel seeds are also used as a mouth freshener after meals.

FENUGREEK is the same as methi seed, which you can generally find in an Indian grocery store (where, incidentally, most spices will be much cheaper than in your general grocery store).

GHEE is clarified butter (pure butter fat without any of the milk solids), and can be bought in Indian grocery stores. It can be heated to much higher temperatures than butter without burning, and has a distinctive flavor.

When a recipe calls for GREEN CHILIES, it's asking for finger hot chilies, which are slender and about a finger-length, with a delicious flavor. (They do ripen to red if left on the plant, and can still be used in these dishes.) These chilies are quite hot, so if you can't find them and substitute in something like jalapeño, you'll want to use more chili. Serrano chilies are a decent substitute; you can also use Thai green chilies for similar heat, but they offer less of the green chili flavor. I store green chilies in the freezer in a big Ziploc bag, and just chop a few of them, still frozen, as needed for Sri Lankan dishes. (Carefully remove the seeds if you're looking for less heat. Wash your hands afterwards!)

IDLI RICE is a specific kind of Indian rice that is parboiled. Parboiled (or converted) rice is rice that has been partially boiled in the husk, through a process of soaking, steaming, and drying. These steps make rice easier to process by hand, boost its nutritional profile (parboiling drives nutrients, especially thiamin, from the bran to the endosperm), and change its texture. (They also reduce its cooking time and make it resistant to weevils.)

JAGGERY is a traditional sugar made from the concentrated sap of palm trees. It comes in a range of shades of brown, and it is delicious. If jaggery is not available, brown sugar + a little molasses will approximate the flavor.

One of the questions I get asked most often is, "Really, *KETCHUP*?" Yes, really. My mother used it, and so can you. If you'd really rather not, though, you can use chopped tomatoes, vinegar, salt, and sugar, cooked down to a sauce. (Which is basically ketchup.)

If you're looking for a fine, fresh, lemony tang with hints of ginger and mint, LEMONGRASS is the herb for you. Buy stalks that are fragrant, tightly formed, and a lemony-green color. If they're loose, brown, or crumbling, they're old and won't lend much flavor to your dish. I often grow lemongrass with my other herbs—since it's a tropical, it does need to come inside for the winter in Chicago! It can also often be found frozen in the grocery store.

You must also have LIME JUICE on hand (lemon may be substituted if lime isn't available), as balancing sweet-salt-tang-spice is key to Sri Lankan cuisine. Too many times when I was first learning to cook, I made a dish, served it to guests, was frustrated that it wasn't quite as tasty as it should be—and realized I'd forgotten to add the lime!

MALDIVE FISH is cured tuna fish, traditionally produced in the Maldives, and is a staple ingredient in Sri Lankan cuisine, acting as a thickening, flavoring, and protein component in vegetable dishes, functioning similarly to the shrimp pastes and fish sauces of southeast Asia. You can use

either of those to substitute if needed, along with Japanese bonito flakes or dried prawns. For seeni sambol, where Maldive fish is a significant ingredient, it's best not to substitute, for the proper flavor.

Many of the recipes call for a little MILK—my mother generally used whole cow's milk, or coconut milk if she was cooking for a party; coconut milk is a little sweeter and much richer in taste due to the high fat content. You can sometimes find light coconut milk, which is not terrible. You can use 2% or 1% or even skim milk; they'll all work fine, as well goat milk—I've also used rice milk, almond milk, and soy milk when cooking for vegans or those with allergies, and while the dish won't thicken quite as much, it still basically works.

I keep a little jar of ground black pepper on hand for dishes that need a teaspoon or more—I buy strongly-flavored Tellicherry PEPPERCORNS from Penzeys online (www.penzeys.com), grind them in a coffee grinder I keep dedicated for spices (although you can use a regular coffee grinder if you clean it out thoroughly), and grind up a jar's worth as needed. The flavor is much better than you'd get from the pre-ground black pepper at the grocery store.

My friend Roshani cooks many of her dishes using RAMPÉ, which is also known as pandan leaf; I never got in the habit of cooking with it, as it was quite hard to find when I was learning to cook. But it's commonly used in Sri Lankan cooking, and a simple way to add it is to drop a leaf into a pot of rice while cooking, where it will lend a lovely aroma; you can also add a few pieces to a curry.

If you don't have ROSE ESSENCE, you can substitute ROSE WATER, which is more readily available in stores. It contains a lot more water, obviously, so adjust other ingredients for pleasing result. Just be careful—the essence is extremely strong. A rough conversion is 5ml rose essence = 15ml rose water, or 1 tsp. rose essence = 1 Tbsp. rose water. You can also buy rose essence online.

There are many recipes for South Indian SAMBAR POWDER available online, but I admit, this one I buy pre-mixed. It's typically a blend of chili, coriander, curry leaves, fenugreek, chana dal, cumin, peppercorn, asafetida, and similar spices.

TAMARIND, a tangy fruit, comes in many forms—blocks of hard paste, fresh pods, dried pods—and the form I prefer, a soft concentrated paste which comes in a small jar (generally with a red lid). Again, the Indian grocery store is your friend.

When soaked in water, the seeds of several basil varieties (TULSI SEEDS) become gelatinous, and are used in Sri Lankan (and other Asian) drinks and desserts, such as falooda.

URAD DAL is also known as black gram / matpe bean / ulunththu. The product sold as BLACK LENTIL is usually the whole urad bean, whereas the split bean (the interior being white) is called WHITE LENTIL. It should not be confused with the much smaller true black lentil (*Lens culinaris*). Generally in these recipes, I'll be using split urad dal, which has been washed and the husks removed; it appears primarily white in color.

VINEGAR is another way to add that characteristic tang to Sri Lankan dishes. White vinegar is standard, though these days, rice wine vinegar is also widely used, with its subtle, delicately sweet flavor. Some Sri Lankan cooks today will even use sushi vinegar, to get that additional sweet note to a dish without the extra step of adding sugar.

MASTER RECIPE:
Sri Lankan Curry Powder

One of the main characteristics of Sri Lankan cooking is that the spices are dark roasted. You cannot simply substitute yellow curry powder! If your local Indian grocery store carries Jaffna Curry Powder, that's from northern Sri Lanka and an excellent option; it can also be found online. Or you can always make your own.

> 1 cup coriander seeds
> ½ cup cumin seeds
> 1 Tbsp. fennel seeds
> 1 rounded tsp. fenugreek seeds (a.k.a. methi seeds)
> 1 2-inch cinnamon stick
> 1 rounded tsp. whole cloves
> 1 rounded tsp. cardamom seeds
> 2 Tbsp. dried curry leaves
> 2 rounded tsp. cayenne

1. In a dry pan over medium heat, roast separately the coriander, cumin, fennel, and fenugreek, stirring constantly until each one becomes a fairly dark brown.

   Note: Do not attempt to save time by roasting them together—they each have different cooking times and you will only end up half-cooking some and burning others.

2. Put into blender container (I use a coffee grinder that is dedicated solely to spice grinding) together with cinnamon stick broken in pieces, the cloves, cardamom, and curry leaves.

3. Blend at high speed until finely powdered. Sieve into a bowl, discarding any large pieces, and combine with cayenne; stir well. Store in airtight jar.

MASTER RECIPE:
Sri Lankan Seasoned Onions

Many of our dishes start with cooking onions in ghee with ginger, garlic, black mustard seed, and cumin seed, so I wanted to take the time to go through that process in a little more detail. Do chop the onions finely; they'll be breaking down to make the base for your sauce, and if they're in big pieces, they'll take much longer to break down into a proper sauce.

A great time-saver, if you're making my curries often, is to do a double (or triple, or quadruple) batch of this, maybe on a lazy Sunday, and then divide and freeze the extra. It means that on a weekday night when you're in a hurry, you can grab a frozen bag of seasoned onions, toss them in a hot pan, and within minutes be adding your meat or vegetables, cutting your weeknight cooking time in half.

Also, you can buy chopped ginger-garlic paste in the Indian stores, which is helpful for when you're in a hurry—I'd use about 2 tablespoons in this recipe. It's not quite as good as chopping fresh, but is an acceptable substitute for everyday cooking.

3 medium yellow onions, chopped fine
3 Tbsp. ghee or vegetable oil
1-2 Tbsp. ginger, chopped fine
1 tsp. black mustard seed
1 tsp. cumin seed
3-5 cloves garlic, chopped fine

Optional first step: Sauté black mustard seed in oil to make mustard oil—this will add an extra little hit of flavor, but I admit, I mostly don't bother with this unless I'm being extra fancy; I add the seeds together later on.

1. Sauté onions in ghee until translucent. Now, you can cook them on high or medium-high, stirring constantly, if you have your other ingredients ready. But I tend to do this step on medium or even low, so I can stir only occasionally, in between chopping ginger, garlic, and any other ingredients.

2. Add black mustard seed, cumin seed, and ginger; sauté a few minutes more. (This is when I'd be chopping my garlic.) If you need more ghee, feel free to add it at this point.

3. Add garlic and cook, stirring occasionally, a few more minutes, until golden-translucent. Garlic burns easily, so you don't want to add it early on, especially when you just have hot oil in the pan. Much safer to add it at this stage.

That's it! You'll almost always be adding fresh curry leaves next, with pieces of cinnamon stick, cardamom pods, and cloves, and then going on to cayenne, roasted curry powder, and salt, but this is a good point to pause, divide, and freeze anything you're not using right away. You can also add the other ingredients and freeze at that point, if you're planning to use them for particular curries that call for them. Be sure to squeeze as much air as possible out of the plastic bag, to avoid freezer burn.

My immediate and extended family, at our house in Connecticut

MENU SUGGESTIONS

LIGHT *and* CLASSIC BREAKFAST:
- idiyappam with sothi and pol sambol

WEEKNIGHT SUPPER:
- beef and potato curry with kale sambol, pickled beet salad, and rice

TO DELIGHT CHILDREN:
- bombatoast (for breakfast)
- ginger-garlic chicken or roast barbecue chicken with cauliflower poriyal and rice (for dinner)
- mango lassi (to drink),
- many options for sweets: inippu thosai, mango fluff, milk toffee, marshmallows

TO TAKE ON *a* PICNIC *or* ON *the* ROAD:
- Chinese rolls, patties, prawn vadai, fish cutlets

UNUSUAL TECHNIQUES *to* TRY:
- Appetizers: Chinese rolls, patties, prawn vadai, ribbon sandwiches
- Mains: appam, biryani, idiyappam, kottu roti, pittu, uppuma
- Meat: nargisi kofta

A SMALL DINNER PARTY:
- goat (mutton) curry with deviled potatoes, green bean varai & eggplant sambol
- golden rice pilaf
- mango lassi & chai
- vattalappam or mango fluff for dessert

BRUNCH *with* FRIENDS:
- hoppers and egg hoppers
- seeni sambol and green coconut chutney
- chicken curry or fish curry
- tropical fruit salad with ginger-lime-honey dressing
- mango-passionfruit mimosas

POTLUCK FAVORITES:
- ribbon sandwiches
- deviled chili eggs
- eggplant sambol
- lamb biryani
- milk toffee

My daughter on right (Kaviarasi Whyte), with her friend Maggie.

COCKTAIL PARTY:
- arrack sour, Ceylon sunrise, and mango-passionfruit punch
- Chinese rolls, fish cutlets, prawn vadai
- chicken patties, ribbon sandwiches, tangy shrimp on toast
- milk toffee and marshmallows

VEGETARIAN FEAST *(to feed twenty to thirty):*
- chili-mango cashews, ribbon sandwiches, and vadai
- asparagus poriyal, cabbage varai, cashew curry
- eggplant curry, deviled potatoes, lime-masala mushrooms
- omelette curry and paruppu
- pittu and/or rice
- falooda and mango lassi
- tropical fruit salad and love cake

ROYAL FEAST
(to feed two hundred or so):

Appetizers:
- Chinese rolls, fish cutlets, prawn vadai
- chicken patties and ribbon sandwiches

Our dog, Elinor, waiting patiently for party food to be left unattended

Mains and Sides:
- crab curry, poricha meen, nargisi kofta
- black pork curry and beef smoore
- cashew curry, eggplant with potatoes and pea pods, green mango curry
- cucumber salad, pickled beet salad, bitter gourd sambol
- pol sambol, leeks fried with chili, mango pickle
- lamb biryani, noodles, roti

Desserts:
- All of them!

Kith and Kin

hair, clothes, and kitchen
redolent with roasted spices
cooking deep into the night
with children and husband asleep
this much unchanged, untranslated

I stand over the pan, stirring
low and slow, singing to amuse
myself—haste would destroy
the spell of memory, consanguinity

coriander cumin fennel fenugreek
in order of decreasing amount
cinnamon cloves cardamom
curry leaves and chili powder

if I have to look up the ingredients
every time, am I insufficiently
authentic? eventually, I will grind
knowledge into my bones

Ammama, could you have guessed
your granddaughter would live
half a world away, would structure
love so differently, would pass your
recipes to a thousand strangers?

My paternal grandmother, Regina
Navaratnasingam, with my father,
N.A.C. Mohanraj

in the old days, recipes were hoarded
like gold bangles; a dowry locked
in your mind could not be stolen;
now I give them away, scatter them
like kisses on the networked seas

I suspect it would frighten you,
what a daughter might give away
might lose forever. yet perhaps
the world is changing. a woman
may give herself away, undiminished

trust me. what the seas carried
away, they will return; your children's
children are with you
though at times unrecognizable

bend down your head and breathe
deep, roasting scents tangled in my hair
see—you know me still. some things
come back to you, a thousandfold

APPETIZERS *and* SNACKS

Chili-Mango Cashews / Kari-Maankai Kaju

Chinese Rolls

Curried Mushroom Spread

Curry Buns

Fish (or Ground Beef, or Vegetable) Cutlets

Plain or Prawn Lentil Patties / Kadali or Iraal Vadai

Patties (usually Chicken)

Ribbon Tea Sandwiches (Carrot, Beet, and Spinach)

Tangy Shrimp on Toast

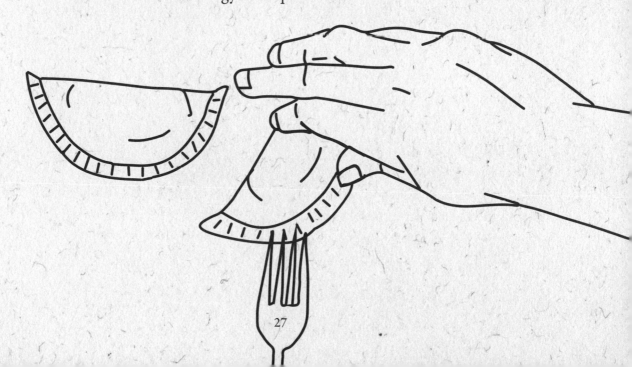

Chili-Mango Cashews /
Kari-Maankai Kaju

(10 minutes + drying time, makes 12 servings)

2 cups dried mango slices, chopped (kitchen shears or food processor recommended)
2 cups roasted, salted cashews, chopped
1-2 Tbsp. butter
1-2 tsp. cayenne
1 tsp. Sri Lankan curry powder
1-2 tsp. crumbled jaggery or brown sugar
enough water to make a glaze
salt or sugar to taste

1. Line a flat cookie sheet or tray with foil; set aside.

2. In a dry pan on medium-high, toast cashews for a few minutes, stirring, until nuts smell yummy.

3. Add butter, cayenne, curry powder, sugar / jaggery, and some water to make a thin glaze. Turn down to medium, and stir for a few minutes until nuts are nicely coated and cooked. (Stir continuously, or nuts will burn.)

4. Stir in mango bits until well combined. Taste (carefully, as it will be hot!), add salt / sugar as desired.

5. Spread flat on foil-lined tray to cool.

Chinese Rolls

(3 hours, makes 50)

Chinese rolls (whether made with meat, chicken, or vegetarian) are an essential Sri Lankan party food. People look forward to them with anticipation, and greet their arrival with glee. They're also a sign of love—in college and after, whenever I visited home, my mother or one of my aunts would make sure that when I left again, it was with a bag of freshly-fried rolls. It was sometimes a little challenging managing the still-steaming bag on the airplane, but it was the sort of gift that was impossible to turn down—made with love and labor, and eventually consumed with delight.

I believe they're called Chinese rolls because they look a little like Chinese egg rolls; during colonial times, Chinese laborers were brought to Sri Lanka and settled there in a small but significant minority community; I assume this dish was invented then. They taste nothing like egg rolls, though.

Growing up, my sisters and I would often be pressed into service for the various stages of roll-making, all sitting around the dining table and working. My mother and aunts made them in a group as well. Especially if doing a larger batch, I highly encourage cooking this dish as a group activity (perhaps inviting a few select friends to come a few hours before your party), which will speed things up by as much as an hour. The final step is best done right before serving.

Portion and serving suggestion:
For a cocktail or other large-ish party, I'd aim for two rolls per guest. It's a filling, rich treat. The recipe scales up or down easily—my mother would generally make

200 at a time, or more, for the Sri Lankan-American parties of my childhood, when immigrant families would gather, hungry for a taste of home. The dish is complex and labor-intensive enough that I wouldn't normally make rolls for a small dinner party, but you certainly could serve them as an appetizer, allowing two per person. Simply divide the recipe as needed.

Note: There are several points in the process where you can pause, refrigerate or freeze, and pick up again later. This is tremendously helpful when prepping for a party—you can do the bulk of the work days, weeks, or even months in advance, as long as you plan appropriately.

For the filling:
- 6 medium onions, chopped fine
- ¼ cup vegetable oil + ½ cup vegetable oil
- ¼ tsp. black mustard seed
- ¼ tsp. cumin seed
- 1-2 Tbsp. cayenne
- 1 Tbsp. Sri Lankan curry powder
- 2 lbs. ground beef (or goat, or chicken)
- ⅓ cup ketchup
- 3 Tbsp. Worcestershire sauce
- 1 tsp. salt + 1 tsp. salt
- 3 medium russet potatoes, diced in roughly ½ -inch cubes

Note: For a vegetarian filling, see the cutlets recipe.

For the crepes:
- 4 cups cold water
- 2 cups milk
- 2 tsp. salt
- 2 eggs
- 4 cups of all-purpose flour

For frying:
> 2 egg whites
> 2 cups breadcrumbs
> 4 cups vegetable oil

1. In a large frying pan, sauté onions in ¼ cup oil on medium-high with mustard seed and cumin seeds until onions are golden / translucent (not brown). Add cayenne and cook 1 minute. Immediately add curry powder, ground beef, ketchup, Worcestershire sauce, and 1 teaspoon salt. Sauté until cooked through. Drain any excess oil, transfer to a large bowl, and let cool. (You can refrigerate for a few days or freeze for up to six months here.)

2. In a clean frying pan, heat ¼ cup oil and fry potato cubes with 1 teaspoon salt on medium-high, stirring, until cooked through. Drain any excess oil and let cool. (You can refrigerate or freeze here—to best preserve potato texture for freezing, spread them out in a flat sheet and freeze, then transfer to large plastic sealable bags.)

3. Combine meat and potato mixture. (You can refrigerate or freeze here.)

4. Make crepes: Combine crepe filling ingredients and mix thoroughly until it forms a thin pancake batter. Heat an 8-inch non-stick frying pan and grease with a little oil between each pancake. Pour a ladle full of batter into the pan and swirl it around gently until it forms a thin pancake. Cook until set without browning; flip and briefly cook other side. Remove and stack on a plate. (If you have a friend with you, you can do steps 4 and 5 together, one making the crepes while the other fills. If you make them ahead of time, separate the crepes with wax paper.)

5. Place a cooked pancake on a plate and add about 2 tablespoons of filling.

6. Proceed to roll the pancake like an egg roll.

Note: Try eating one or two at this stage (not required, but recommended, as there's something deliciously unctuous about them, and I always used to steal some at this point when rolling for my mom).

7. In a small bowl, beat 2 egg whites. Set up a plate piled with breadcrumbs. Dip rolls in egg mixture, then roll in breadcrumbs, then remove to a separate plate. (Don't pile them up, as they'll squish—use multiple clean plates.) Continue until all rolls are encased in breadcrumbs. (This is also a good place to pause and freeze them.)

8. Heat vegetable oil in a large pan until quite hot, then, using a Chinese spider (mesh metal spoon) (recommended) or spatula, fry until golden, removing to separate plates lined with paper towels. (I usually turn the heat down a little after the first batch, which helps avoid burning them.) Serve hot as an appetizer, with a little spicy sauce (MD sauce can be found online, and is a classic choice) as accompaniment if desired.

Curried Mushroom Spread

(30 minutes, serves dozens)

This dish is entirely my own invention; I became frustrated trying to have dinner parties, because so many of our short eats are deep-fried—delicious, but not so good for you. This didn't actually end up being all that healthy, given the cream. Ah well.

> 2 lbs. mushrooms, chopped fine
> 2 large onions, chopped fine
> several Tbsp. butter—add as needed
> 1-2 rounded tsp. Sri Lankan curry powder
> ¼ - ½ cup thick coconut milk or heavy cream
> ½ tsp. lime juice
> salt and pepper to taste

1. Sauté onions in butter until golden; add mushrooms and sauté on high heat, reducing as much liquid as possible. Add more butter as necessary. When mushrooms are well-reduced, add curry powder, salt, and pepper; mix well.

2. Add coconut milk or cream, turn down heat to low, and simmer until well blended and cream is reduced, about 5-10 minutes. Add lime juice, check seasonings, adjust if needed. Remove from heat and let cool. Ready to use at this point.

3. For a finer consistency, spoon mixture into food processor and pulse until well blended; it's now suitable for mounding on crackers, or using in tea sandwiches.

Note: Mango-ginger chutney mixed with cream cheese is also a tasty cracker spread, and ham or grilled chicken + mango-ginger chutney makes excellent tea sandwiches.

Curry Buns (Meat or Vegetable) / Mas Paan

(2 ½ hours for cooking curry, rising the dough, and baking, makes 30 buns)

Mas Paan is literally 'meat bread,' and is a favorite snack sold at roadside stands, hotel cafes, and transit stations across Sri Lanka. The yeast bread may be filled with whatever curry you like—fish and vegetarian options are also common. Having thirty mas paan in my fridge and freezer means that I'll snack happy for a few days, take them with me while traveling—they're great to have on the road—and be able to pull some out of the freezer to toast up when I get home again. They're best piping hot, but may also be happily eaten at room temperature.

Note: If you don't want to make the dough by hand, and your grocery store carries frozen loaves of bread dough, I've thawed and used a pair of those for this recipe to good effect.

1 recipe portion of beef and potato curry or other curry
½ c. milk
3 tsp. sugar
2 ½ tsp. salt
3 oz. butter
1 ½ c. warm water
1 packet (about 2 ¼ tsp.) active dry yeast
5 ½ – 6 c. all-purpose or bread flour

1. Make curry, if needed; it's tempting to make it while the dough is proving, but the timing can be tricky, since the curry needs to cool down, and your dough may overprove, turning yeasty. (I admit to risking it on occasion, though, for efficiency's sake.) The curry should be cooked until it is very dry, and then cooled down to room temperature.

2. Make dough: Scald milk, stir in sugar, salt, and butter and cool to lukewarm. Measure warm water into a large bowl; stir yeast into water until dissolved. Add milk mixture and 3 c. of flour; beat until smooth. Add enough flour to make a soft dough. Turn onto a lightly floured board, and knead until smooth and elastic, about ten minutes. Grease a bowl with butter, then put the dough ball in, turning it to make sure it's all greased. Cover with plastic wrap or a cloth and allow to prove in a warm place until doubled in bulk (inside a turned off oven works well), about 1 – 1.5 hours. Divide the dough into 30 equal portions.

3. Flatten each portion to a circle (thinner at the edges), put a spoonful of beef and potato curry in the center, and bring the edges together, pressing to seal, creating a round bun.

4. Put buns join–downwards on greased baking trays, with a little space between them to allow for rising and spreading. Cover with a dry cloth and leave in a warm place for 30-40 minutes or until nearly doubled in bulk.

5. Brush with egg glaze and bake at 400° until golden brown, about 10 minutes. Can be served hot or cold. Lovely with hot, sweet, milky tea.

Fish (or Ground Beef, or Vegetable) Cutlets

(90 minutes, makes about 50)

There's a part of my mind (formed in childhood over monthly Sri Lankan birthday parties at various aunties' homes) that says a party isn't properly a party unless there are rolls and cutlets. So when people agree to come over to my house and let me feed them rolls and cutlets, it makes that childhood bit of me very happy.

Some Americans find these too fishy, but I love them. Over the years, my family has come up with adaptations to suit the tastes of those (like Kevin) who dislike fish, and they've even come up with a variation for vegetarians. But honestly, the mackerel ones are the tastiest. I wouldn't recommend attempting this recipe unless you're willing to get your hands dirty (and fishy-smelling)—you really need to work the filling with your hand to blend and shape it properly.

2 cans of mackerel, 15 oz. each
2 large russet potatoes
4 medium onions, chopped fine, for sautéing
1 tsp. black mustard seed
1 tsp. cumin seed
2 Tbsp. oil or ghee
1 rounded tsp. salt
⅔ cup lime juice
2 small onions, minced, for mixing in

4 rounded tsp. fresh green chilies, chopped fine
1 rounded tsp. ground black pepper
2 eggs, beaten
dry breadcrumbs, for coating
oil for deep frying

1. Drain fish thoroughly, removing as much liquid as possible. While fish are draining, boil the potatoes, peel, and mash them. Clean the fish, removing skin and bones, and break it into small pieces.

2. Sauté the four fine-chopped medium onions in oil with cumin and black mustard seed until golden-translucent. Add fish, salt, and lime juice, then cook until very dry (this process reduces the fishy smell, and the drier you get the mixture, the less excess oil they'll pick up when frying). Let cool.

3. Using your clean hand, mix thoroughly the fish, mashed potatoes, the two small minced raw onions, black pepper, and chilies until a fairly smooth paste. Shape the mixture into small balls, about the size of a cupped palm. I squeeze the mixture in my balled hand as I go, compressing so the resulting ball is nice and firm—that helps it keep its form when frying. (You can pause, cover with plastic wrap, and refrigerate at this point if making a day or two ahead.)

4. Roll each ball in beaten egg, and then roll each ball in the dry breadcrumbs. (You can freeze at this point if making ahead—spread them out on a flat cookie sheet so they're not touching and freeze them—once frozen, you can pack them more tightly in gallon Ziploc bags, and they should hold their shape. They'll be fine in the freezer for weeks, which helps when you're prepping for a big party; you can either fry them frozen or spread them out on plates and let them thaw first.)

5. Fry a few at a time in deep hot oil over medium-high heat—not too hot, or they'll start to break apart! This should take a minute or so each. When well-browned, lift out with a slotted spoon and drain on a metal rack placed over a tray lined with a few layers of paper towels.

For ground beef cutlets: For 2 lbs. lean ground beef, when you sauté the 4 chopped onions, add 1-2 heaping teaspoon red Indian cayenne and ½ cup ketchup, as well as the rounded teaspoon salt from above. Add the ground beef (skipping the lime juice), and fry until very dry, draining any excess oil. Skip the raw onion, chilies, and black pepper—proceed otherwise as for the fish cutlets.

For vegetable cutlets: Just use 1 lb. frozen mixed vegetables, thawed (you might have to cut up the green beans into smaller pieces). Sauté the onions, mustard seed, and cumin seed as for the fish; add the vegetables and salt and cook until very dry. Skip the raw onion if you like, but definitely stir in an extra ½ teaspoon of salt when you mix the veggies in with the potatoes, black pepper, and chilies. Proceed otherwise as for the fish cutlets. Using panko breadcrumbs works beautifully here, lending interesting texture and a light, crispy crunch.

Plain or Prawn Lentil Patties / Kadalai or Iraal Vadai

(45 minutes, plus 2 hours lentil soaking time, makes about 24-30)

When you go visiting in Sri Lanka, your hosts will often insist on quickly frying up some vadai for you, accompanied by hot, sweet, milky tea. You can protest once, for politeness's sake, that they shouldn't go to the trouble. Then say yes.

Vadai typically don't refrigerate and reheat well; they're best served hot, right after frying, but are also tasty at room temperature. Vadai are a perfect mid-afternoon snack with tea or coffee or mango-passionfruit juice; they also make a terrific picnic or road-trip food.

1 cup split red lentils / masoor dal
8 oz. prawns (if using)
1 large onion, chopped
3 green chilies, chopped
3 dried red chilies, broken into small pieces
1 Tbsp. ginger, minced
3 cloves garlic
1 dozen curry leaves
1 tsp. cumin seeds
1 tsp. fennel seeds
1 tsp. salt
oil for deep frying
rice flour if needed

1. Soak lentils for at least two hours. (Can be done overnight.) Drain.

2. Wash and devein the prawns and set aside; you can shell them if you prefer, but usually you just eat the crispy fried shell too.

   Note: People often prefer a more coarse texture to their vadai—for that, set aside half the lentils and/or the chopped onions before the next step, and just mix them back in after grinding, to preserve more texture. I'm a bit of an outlier in that I like my vadai to be more finely-textured.

3. Add the lentils to food processor with other ingredients; grind coarsely, scraping down the sides with a rubber spatula once or twice so they're well blended.

4. Set oil to heating. While it heats, mold the mixture into small balls (if the dough is too wet to mold, add rice flour 1-2 tablespoon at a time, until it reaches a workable texture). Flatten them into patties.

5. For plain vadai, gently slip into the hot oil and deep fry both sides, until crisp and golden brown. (My husband doesn't like seafood, poor man, so I make the plain vadai first, so as not to flavor the oil, and then the prawn ones after.) For prawn vadai, press a prawn into each patty and gently slip into the oil. (If you use large prawns, it'll be difficult to keep the round shape of the patty, but personally, I'm fine with a more irregular patty if it means big, beautiful, crispy prawns.)

6. Remove with slotted spoon and drain on paper towel. Serve hot or at room temperature; they can be eaten straight up, but I like to add a little mint-cilantro chutney or mango pickle. They're also commonly served with other chutneys, pickles, sambar, or yogurt.

Patties (usually Chicken)

(2 hours, makes about 30)

These are classic short-eats; patties can also be made with a mix of meats—chicken, beef, and pork work well together. The filling may be made in advance and frozen if desired, or you can go all the way to filling the patties and then freeze them in layers, with sheets of parchment paper to separate, before the final frying step. That makes it easier to manage prep for a big party. Allow patties to thaw completely before frying.

Patty pastry:
> 2 cups plain flour
> ½ rounded tsp. salt
> 3 Tbsp. butter
> ¼ cup thick coconut milk
> 2 egg yolks, beaten (reserve whites)
> peanut oil for frying

Filling:
> 2 ½ lbs. boneless chicken thighs
> 2 Tbsp. ghee or vegetable oil
> 1 medium onion, chopped fine
> 8 curry leaves, on the stalk if possible
> 2 rounded tsp. Sri Lankan curry powder

1 rounded tsp. ground turmeric
¼ rounded tsp. ground cloves
¼ rounded tsp. ground cinnamon
½ rounded tsp. ground black pepper
2 rounded tsp. salt
2 strips lemon rind (or roughly that amount of lemongrass)
½ cup thick coconut milk
1-2 lightly-beaten egg whites for sealing pastry (or water)

1. Make filling. Put chicken into a saucepan with just enough water to cover, bring to a boil, cover, and simmer for 20 minutes. Cool chicken, remove from pot (reserving stock), and mince. (In a food processor is fine.)

2. Heat ghee in a saucepan and fry the onion and curry leaves until onion is soft and starts to brown. (Leaving curry leaves on the stalk will make it easier to remove them at the end.) Add the curry powder, turmeric, cloves, cinnamon, pepper, and salt and stir well. Add about 1 ½ cups of the leftover stock. Add lemongrass and the minced chicken. Mix well and simmer gently until chicken is tender and liquid almost evaporated.

3. Add coconut milk, stir, and cook uncovered until coconut milk is absorbed.

4. Remove from heat. When cool, pick out the lemon rind or lemongrass and the curry leaves.

5. Make pastry: Sift flour and salt into a bowl and rub in the butter with your fingertips. Add the coconut milk and egg yolks mixed together and knead lightly to a smooth dough. If necessary, add a little extra milk or flour.

6. Wrap dough in parchment paper and chill for 30 minutes.

7. Take one quarter of the dough at a time and roll out very thinly on lightly floured board. Cut into circles using a large cookie cutter about 3 inches in diameter.

8. Put a teaspoonful of the filling on the pastry rounds. Wet the edges of the pastry with egg white or water, fold over to make half circle, and press edges firmly together to seal. Ornament the edge by pressing with a key or the tines of a fork.

9. When all the patties are made, fry a few at a time in deep hot oil. Drain on layers of paper towels and serve warm. Can be made ahead and refrigerated (or frozen)—reheat in a 350° oven.

Ribbon Tea Sandwiches
(Carrot, Beet, and Spinach)

(1 ½ hours, serves dozens)

These are a favorite across Sri Lanka, and are made with a variety of vegetables—some use asparagus instead of spinach, for example. They are quite ridiculously pretty, with their contrasting stripes of color, and are a staple at Christmas parties and other festive events. They are just a little spicy, but spice levels may be adjusted up or down, as desired. I like mine tangy, but if you don't like tang, leave out the vinegar, and they will still be quite tasty.

Note: These are quite time-consuming to assemble; I usually try to make sure I have at least an extra pair of hands to help at that stage.

½ pound carrots, peeled and coarsely chopped
½ pound beets, peeled and coarsely chopped
1 10 oz. packet frozen chopped spinach, thawed, with the excess
 water squeezed out
3 green chilies
1 8 oz. package cream cheese
1 stick butter
1 cup mayonnaise
1 ½ tsp. onion powder
1 ½ tsp. garlic powder

¾ tsp. white pepper (black is also fine)

3 Tbsp. vinegar

1 ½ tsp. salt

3 loaves thin white bread (recommended: Pepperidge Farms Sandwich Bread or Very Thin, if you can find it.)

Note: Each sandwich uses 4 slices of bread. Each large sandwich will be cut into four bite-size sandwiches.

1. Chop carrots finely in food processor with one green chili. Add ⅓ package cream cheese, ⅓ stick butter, and ⅓ cup mayo. Add ½ teaspoon onion powder, ½ teaspoon garlic powder, ¼ teaspoon white pepper, 1 tablespoon vinegar, and ½ teaspoon salt. Combine until smooth, taste seasonings and adjust if desired, and transfer spread to a separate bowl. Rinse out food processor.

2. Repeat process with beets + chili, and then again with spinach + chili.

3. Spread carrot mixture on a slice of bread. Place second slice of bread on top and spread with beet mixture. Place third slice of bread on top and spread with spinach mixture. Place final slice of bread on top. Using a serrated bread knife, gently cut off the crusts.

Cut each large sandwich into four triangles. (I recommend cleaning the blade between cuts with a wet paper towel if you want to avoid beet mixture staining the bread.) Arrange beautifully on a plate and serve.

Note: If not serving immediately, place in a large storage container and lay a moist paper towel on top of the sandwiches to keep them fresh. Alternatively, you can prepare the sandwiches the night before, not cutting them, wrap each large sandwich individually in plastic wrap, and then cut them when you're ready to serve. That does take quite a bit of plastic wrap, though! Thanks to Roshani Anandappa for walking me through this process.

Note 2: When I cut off the crusts, I save them and throw the bag of crusts in the freezer. And then, when I'm feeling like cozy comfort food, I take some leftover curry, stir in the crusts (still frozen is fine), and sauté it for oh, five minutes or so, until the bread has sopped up all the liquid. Essentially a Sri Lankan version of a hot panzanella. Yummy and comforting.

Tangy Shrimp on Toast

(30 minutes, serves dozens)

My mother is known for these delicious, fussy little appetizers. They present beautifully for a cocktail party.

> 1 lb. raw medium shrimp, peeled
> 2 medium onions, minced
> enough vegetable oil to sauté (about 3 Tbsp.)
> 1-2 rounded tsp. cayenne
> ketchup to taste (about ¼ cup)
> 1 tsp. lime juice
> ½ - 1 rounded tsp. salt
> cilantro or curly parsley for garnish
> either buttery crackers or slices of white bread
> butter to spread
> mustard to spread (optional)

Optional: Cut small circles of white bread and toast in an oven for a few minutes. Spread with butter, or butter mixed with mustard. Alternately, use crackers.

1. Sauté onions in oil until golden; add cayenne and sauté on high a minute or two until darkened.

2. Add shrimp, ketchup, lime juice, and salt; turn down heat to medium and cook, stirring, until well blended.

3. Serve on toast or crackers, placing 1-2 pieces of shrimp on each one and garnishing with a sprig of parsley or cilantro.

EGGS, POULTRY, *and* MEAT

EGGS

Deviled Eggs

Egg Curry / Muttai Kari

Omelette

Omelette Curry

Eggs in Meatballs / Scotch Eggs / Nargisi (Narcissus) Kofta

CHICKEN

Braised Pepper Chicken

Chicken Curry / Kozhi Kari

Deviled Chicken

Ginger / Garlic Chicken

Roast Barbecue Chicken

Fried Liver Curry / Eeral Kari

PORK *and* LAMB

Black Pork Curry / Panri Iraichchi Kari / Padre Kari

Goat (Mutton) Curry / Aattu Iraichchi Kari

Lamb Curry / Semmari Aattu Iraichchi Kari

Meatball Curry / Frikkadel

BEEF

Beef Smoore / Mas Ismoru

Beef and Potato Curry

Tangy Peppered Beef Stew

BASIC PROCESS *for* POULTRY *and* MEAT CURRIES

The base process for a meat or poultry curry is the same—essentially, you sauté chopped onions, ginger, and garlic in oil or ghee, with black mustard seed, cumin seed, and curry leaves. When the onions are softened and golden-translucent (but not overly-browned), you add cayenne, curry powder, ketchup, salt, and the meat of your choice. Cook until done, adding a half-cup of milk and/or a teaspoon of lime juice at the end to balance the flavors.

You can use beef, lamb, pork, goat (which, confusingly, Sri Lankans call "mutton"), or chicken. I strongly recommend using meat with good fat marbling (such as beef chuck roast, or pork shoulder), and chicken thighs rather than breast.

If you and your guests are willing to eat meat on the bone, cooking it bone-in will make for a better flavor—but admittedly, eating that way can be a bit tricky if you're eating with a fork instead of your hands. Sometimes I will cut the meat off the bones beforehand, but still put the bones in to simmer with the sauce. But if I'm in a hurry, boneless meat works just fine.

You can cook the meat curries in thirty minutes to an hour, but if you have the time to let the meats simmer on low heat for two hours, they will reward you with a richer sauce.

Note on cooking with alcohol: Sri Lankan traditional food doesn't typically use alcohol, but I've found that adding a bit to a meat dish will often enhance the flavors. So don't hesitate to add a half-cup to cup of wine to a pot of beef or lamb; for a pork dish, I'd typically add half a bottle of hard apple cider—and drink the other half while stirring. As they say—one for the pot, one for the chef!

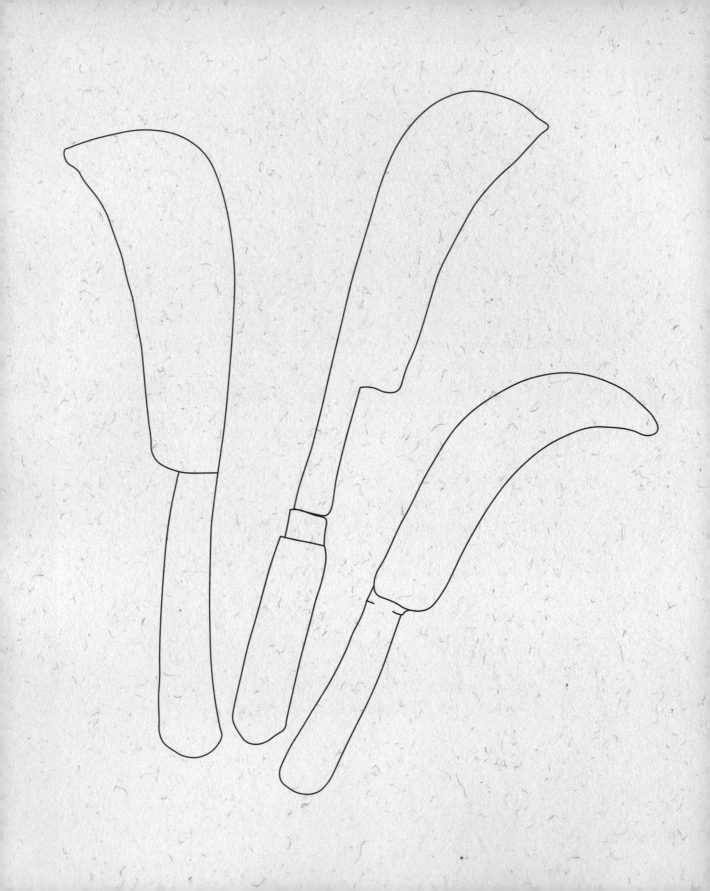

Deviled Chili Eggs

(20 minutes, serves 8)

This is not what Westerners call deviled eggs! It's one of the first dishes I learned to make; very simple, can be made quickly, terrific to serve to vegetarians, and adds a nice punch of pungent spice to your meal. This is a great last-minute addition to a dinner party menu, for that moment when you're panicking about whether you've made enough food. As a bonus, the deviled onions are excellent as a condiment on their own, added to a grilled chicken sandwich, for example.

3 medium onions, sliced
3 Tbsp. vegetable oil
1 tsp. black mustard seed
1 tsp. cumin seed
2 Tbsp. (or more to taste) cayenne
3 Tbsp. ketchup
1 rounded tsp. salt
8 eggs

1. Boil eggs. There are many recommended methods for boiling eggs—I start them in cold water, bring it to a boil, turn it off, put a lid on, and leave for fifteen minutes.

2. While eggs are boiling, sauté onions in oil on high with mustard seed and cumin seeds until onions are golden / translucent (not brown).

3. Add cayenne and cook 1 minute. Immediately add ketchup and salt; stir until well blended and cooked through, about 5 minutes. Remove from heat.

4. When eggs are cooked, shell and slice in half. Arrange on a plate and spoon chili onions over, turning gently to coat.

Egg Curry / Muttai Kari

(30 minutes, serves 4)

A classic egg curry, creamy and mild. A nice option for adding protein to a vegetarian meal.

8 eggs
1 bag pearl onions (or 2-3 regular onions)
4 cloves garlic, chopped
½ tsp. fenugreek seed
1 tsp. cumin seed
1 tsp. black mustard seed
1 tsp. salt
1 tsp. ground turmeric
1 tsp. Sri Lankan curry powder
1 dozen curry leaves
2 cups coconut milk
½ cup roasted cashews
½ cup sultanas (golden raisins)

1. Hard-boil eggs; cool and peel. While eggs are cooling, peel and quarter a bag of pearl onions. (Alternatively, chop 2-3 regular onions.)

2. Sauté onions in a few
    tablespoons of ghee (or
    butter, or oil). Add garlic
    along with spices; stir to
    combine. Add coconut
    milk, cashews, and
    sultanas; simmer until
    reduced to a nice sauce.

3. Halve the eggs and slip
    them into the sauce.
    Serve warm with rice or
    bread.

Omelette

(15 minutes, serves 4)

A Sri Lankan omelette is typically filled with onion and green chili, and seasoned with salt and pepper. You can adjust the amount of green chilies to your preferred heat level; I'd consider this medium spicy. This dish works equally well as scrambled eggs, if you don't feel like making an omelette, and can be served with buttered toast for a light breakfast, or with rice and curries for a more substantial meal.

6 eggs, well-beaten
1 tsp. ground black pepper
¾ tsp. salt
1 onion, chopped fine
3 green chilies, chopped fine
6 curry leaves, chopped (optional)
1-2 Tbsp. vegetable oil, ghee, or butter
1 tomato, chopped

1. Mix black pepper and salt into the eggs.

2. Sauté onion, green chili, and curry leaves in oil until golden. Spread evenly in pan and turn heat to medium.

3. Pour egg mixture over onion mixture, add chopped tomato, and make omelette as you normally would.

4. Portion omelette into pieces and serve.

Note: Omelette pieces can also be slipped into curry sauce to make omelette curry.

Omelette Curry

(15 minutes + omelette time, serves 4)

Leftover omelettes? This is what you do with them.

> 2 onions, chopped fine
> 1 Tbsp. ginger, minced
> 3 cloves garlic , sliced
> ½ tsp. black mustard seed
> ½ tsp. cumin seed
> 6-12 curry leaves (optional)
> 2-3 Tbsp. oil or ghee
> 1 tsp. cayenne
> 1 tsp. Sri Lankan curry powder
> 1 tsp. salt
> 2 cups coconut milk
> omelette pieces (made from 6 eggs)
> 1-2 tsp. lime juice to taste

1. Sauté onions, ginger, garlic, mustard seed, cumin seed, and curry leaves in oil until golden.

2. Add cayenne and cook for a few seconds, then add curry powder, salt, and coconut milk. Bring to a boil, then turn down to medium and cook for 5-10 minutes, until well blended.

3. Add lime juice, taste, and adjust seasonings as needed. Sauce should be the consistency of gravy; not too thick, not too thin. Add liquid or cook down as needed, as you won't be able to adjust it further after adding the egg.

4. Slip in the omelette pieces, reduce heat to low, and simmer a few more minutes. Serve with rice or bread.

Note: This also works well with hard-boiled egg halves instead of omelette pieces.

Eggs in Meatballs / Scotch Eggs / Nargisi (Narcissus) Kofta

(2 hours, serves 6)

This elegant dish made its way down to Sri Lanka from India, where it was a favorite in the Mughal court. Known as Scotch Eggs in Europe, the British store Fortnum & Mason claims to have invented this dish in 1738, but given how prevalent kofta are throughout South Asia and the Middle East, it seems more likely that the dish travelled from East to West, rather than the reverse. They take their name from the white-and-yellow varieties of narcissus flowers (a.k.a. daffodils).

Nargisi kofta lend themselves to different variations—you can use chicken eggs or adorable little quail eggs, you can use lamb or beef, you can gild them in saffron for a fancier presentation and a subtle added flavor, you can fry them and take them along whole on your picnic, or you can slice them and serve them in a curry sauce, rich with tomato, yogurt, and cilantro. All the options are good!

Meatballs:
- 14 quail eggs or 7 chicken eggs
- 1 lb. twice-minced* lamb or beef
- 1 small onion, chopped fine
- 3 cloves garlic, minced
- ½ tsp. fresh ginger, finely grated
- 1 tsp. salt

1 tsp. Sri Lankan curry powder (or garam masala)

½ tsp. ground turmeric

½ cup water

3 Tbsp. chickpea flour (may substitute regular flour)

oil for frying

1 tsp. saffron powder for gilding (optional) (grind threads to make
  powder if needed)

Curry sauce:

2 Tbsp. ghee or vegetable oil

1 tsp. cumin seed

1 tsp. black mustard seed

1 medium onion, chopped fine

3 cloves garlic, minced

2 tsp. ginger, minced

1 tsp. Sri Lankan curry powder

1 tsp. ground turmeric

½ - 1 tsp. cayenne

1 15 oz. can chopped tomatoes

1 tsp. salt

½ - 1 cup yogurt

fresh cilantro leaves, chopped, to garnish

* *Your butcher can twice-mince the meat for you, or you can do it at home in a food processor; I recommend chilling the bowl and blade first. Your goal is a fine, even mince, with the fat distributed well through the meat.*

1. Boil 12 quail eggs (or 6 chicken eggs). (If you stir them constantly for the first five minutes of simmering, that will help center the yolks, making for a prettier presentation.) Let cool, then shell and set aside.

2. Combine meat in a saucepan with onion, garlic, ginger, salt, curry powder, turmeric, and water. Stir well and cook on medium, covered, until meat is well cooked, about 20-30 minutes. (If there is a large amount of oil, you may want to skim some off at this point.) Add flour and continue cooking until all the liquid has been absorbed. Let cool, and mix with your clean hand until very smooth.

3. Beat remaining egg(s) and mix in saffron. Mold meat mixture around hard-boiled eggs (I find that one meat-enclosed quail egg just fits into my small hand). Dip kofta in beaten egg and fry in hot oil until golden brown; drain on paper towels. Cut in half and serve hot—or reserve while you make sauce.

4. Sauté cumin, mustard, onions, ginger, and garlic in oil until onions are golden. Add curry powder, turmeric, cayenne, and stir for a minute. Then add tomatoes and salt, and cook on medium until well blended and sauce textured (about 15 minutes). Add yogurt to taste. Serve hot with sliced-in-half kofta, garnished with cilantro. Delicious with rice or bread.

Braised Pepper Chicken

(30 minutes, serves 4-6)

This is a milder chicken preparation, only using black pepper, rather than chili.

4 Tbsp. butter, divided 2 and 2

2 medium onions, sliced

3 lbs. chicken, jointed and skinned

3 Tbsp. ginger, minced

3-5 cloves garlic, crushed

1 ½ cups ketchup

1 Tbsp. soy sauce + 1 Tbsp. fish sauce (alternatively, 2 Tbsp.
  Worcestershire sauce)

1-2 tsp. ground black pepper

3 small pieces cinnamon stick

3 cardamom pods

½ cup red wine, optional

½ cup white vinegar

½ cup water

1 tsp. salt

½ cup roast cashews

1. In a large frying pan, sauté onions in 2 tablespoons butter. When golden, remove to a separate bowl.

2. Add chicken and 2 tablespoons butter to pan and cook on high, turning to brown all sides. When golden, remove to a separate bowl.

3. Combine remaining ingredients (except for cashews) in the pan, bring to a boil, turn heat down to medium, and reduce until sauce is thick.

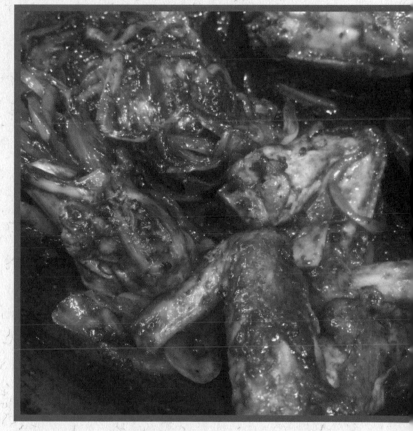

4. Add chicken back to the pan, cover, and cook until chicken is cooked through, about 15-20 minutes. Remove lid and reduce sauce until it thickly coats the chicken.

5. Add onions to the pan and stir until well combined. Serve hot with rice. (Optional: garnish with roast cashews.)

Variation: If making for children at a party, you can use just chicken legs, and skip the onions (and cashews) entirely.

Chicken Curry / Kozhi Kari

(1 hour, serves 6)

This is the classic Sri Lankan chicken dish; if you were just going to make one, this should be the one. A key to a good chicken curry is having a tasty kulambu (or kuzhambu, depending on how you do the transliteration), which is basically the curry sauce or gravy. Some people make it more liquid, some more thick (if you use potatoes in this dish, they will thicken the sauce). In this recipe you build a fairly spicy sauce, and then add whole milk partway through the cooking process, which melds the flavors and mellows the spice level, lending your curry a creamy richness.

You can use other kinds of milk if you'd prefer, and in fact, coconut milk is often used in Sri Lanka, but coconut milk is a little rich for everyday cooking—my family tends to save it for special occasion meals. I've used goat milk (works fine) and soy milk (a little thin, but acceptable). Almond milk is quite thin, and has a distinct nutty flavor—it's not bad, but it does take the curry in a different direction; if you can find cashew milk, that might be a better option.

Note: If you're using coconut milk, which is fairly sweet, you may want to switch out the ketchup for chopped fresh tomatoes + a little vinegar. My mother started using ketchup (which has sugar in it already) to compensate for the lack of sweetness in cow's milk, when she first came to America as an immigrant in 1973, and coconuts and coconut milk were not so easy to come by.

3-5 medium onions, diced

3 Tbsp. vegetable oil

1 tsp. black mustard seed

1 tsp. cumin seed

3 cloves

3 whole cardamom pods

1 cinnamon stick, broken into 3 pieces

1-2 Tbsp. cayenne

1 Tbsp. Sri Lankan curry powder

12 pieces chicken, about 2 ½ lbs., skinned and trimmed of fat

Note: Use legs and thighs—debone if you must, but they'll be tastier cooked on the bone. Don't use breast meat—it's not nearly as tasty. (Alternately, use 6 pieces of chicken and 3 russet potatoes, peeled and cubed.) If you crack the bones (using the back of a heavy knife), it will allow the marrow to add rich flavor to the dish.

⅓ cup ketchup

1 heaping tsp. salt

½ cup milk

1 Tbsp. lime juice

1. In a large pot, sauté onions in oil on medium-high with mustard seed and cumin seed, cloves, cardamom pods, and cinnamon pieces, until onions are golden / translucent (not brown). Add cayenne and cook one minute. Immediately add curry powder, chicken, ketchup, and salt.

2. Lower heat to medium. Cover and cook, stirring periodically, until chicken is cooked through and sauce is thick, about 20 minutes. Add water if necessary to avoid scorching. Add potatoes if using, and add milk, to thicken and mellow spice level; stir until well blended.

3. Cook 20 more minutes, until potatoes are cooked through. Stir in lime juice; serve hot.

Deviled Chicken

(45 minutes + marinating time, serves 6-8)

This same deviled recipe is traditionally adapted for prawns, fish, pork, beef, soya chunks, etc.—any protein. If you want to make it to homestyle levels of truly devilish spice, use 2 teaspoons cayenne, skipping the paprika, and be sure to include the green chilies too. You can also deep-fry the protein instead of pan-frying, which will give a beautifully crispy texture; in that case, remove most of the oil before adding onions, etc. to the pan.

1 tsp. cayenne
1 tsp. paprika
1 tsp. ground turmeric
½ tsp. black pepper
1 tsp. salt
2 tsp. lime juice
6 chicken thighs, deboned and cut into bite-size pieces
1 large onion
2-3 cloves garlic
1 thumb-sized piece of ginger, peeled
1 large tomato
3 green chilies (optional)
3 Tbsp. ketchup
1 red bell pepper (or banana pepper)
vegetable oil for frying
fresh cilantro / lime slices for garnish (optional)

71

1. Mix first five spices and lime juice in a large bowl; add chicken pieces and mix until well coated. Marinate three hours (or overnight).

2. Peel and slice onion. For the ginger and garlic, grate the ginger finely into a bowl (a microplane grater makes this easy). Crush in the garlic. Mix them together. (Alternatively, use 1-2 teaspoons pre-made ginger-garlic paste.) Cut tomato into large chunks. Mince green chilies if using. Chop red bell pepper.

3. Heat oil on high; add chicken and sear, turning to brown all sides. Remove to a large plate.

4. In the same pan, sauté onions, garlic, and ginger in oil on medium-high until golden, stirring. (Add a little water or red wine if needed, to scrape up the delicious fond on the bottom of the pan.)

5. Add green chilies or jalapeños (if desired) and ketchup; cook into a red sauce.

6. Add chicken, bell pepper, and tomatoes to pan and simmer 5-10 minutes, until chicken is cooked through and sauce has thickened. Garnish with chopped fresh coriander and slices of lime. Serve hot, over rice.

Ginger-Garlic Chicken

(30-90 minutes, serves 6-8)

The timing on this is so variable because you can either do it the long way described below, the way my mother recommends, which is definitely a bit tastier—or you can do a much faster version, where you mix the spices with the chicken, skip the marinating, and then just sauté the chicken in the pan on medium-high until cooked through and serve. I use both methods, mostly depending on how much of a hurry I'm in. Regardless of which method you use, this dish is best served fresh; if it sits, the chicken will tend to dry up and not be as tasty.

Note: This is my daughter's favorite chicken dish, and one she always greets with delight; she started eating it when she was about five, with no added cayenne. Over time, I've added a little more cayenne when feeding it to both kids, serving with milk to help them along; you can also use black pepper if you'd prefer.

1 heaping tsp. ginger powder
1 heaping tsp. garlic powder
1 heaping tsp. ground turmeric
1 tsp. salt
12 chicken thighs, about 2 lbs., deboned and cut into bite-size pieces
vegetable oil for frying
½ to 2 heaping tsp. cayenne (to taste, optional)

1. Mix first four spices in a large bowl; add chicken pieces and rub with your hands until well coated. Marinate ½ hour.

2. Heat oil on high; add cayenne (if using) and cook 15 seconds, stirring.

3. Add chicken and sear on high, turning to brown all sides.

4. Reduce heat to low and cover; cook approximately 15-20 minutes, until meat is cooked through.

5. Uncover and cook until all the liquid is gone.

6. Tilt pan and push chicken pieces to one side; allow excess oil to drain to one side for 5 minutes. Remove chicken to dish and serve hot.

Note: If reheating a day or two later, I recommend reheating in a pan with a little coconut milk; just simmer 5-10 minutes, enough for the milk to thicken with the spices into a nice sauce. Or serve dry chicken with a nice coconut-milky vegetable curry, like carrot or beet curry.

Roast Barbecue Chicken

(2 hours, serves 6 adults or 12 kids)

My mother used to host big Sri Lankan parties for a couple hundred people, and she'd often make large trays of barbecue chicken—mild for the kids, spicy for the adults. She would actually just use store-bought barbecue sauce, adding cayenne, which works great, but you can also make your own using the recipe below. You can also throw these on the grill, in which case, you might stir some softened butter into the sauce to help prevent sticking.

1 dozen chicken legs and/or thighs, skins removed
1 tsp. garlic powder
1 tsp. ginger powder
1 tsp. black pepper
1 tsp. ground turmeric
1 tsp. salt

Barbecue sauce:
1 cup ketchup
2 tsp. Worcestershire sauce
2 tsp. dry mustard
2 Tbsp. jaggery or brown sugar
2 Tbsp. vinegar
1-2 tsp. cayenne (optional)

1. Prick chicken pieces with a fork, rub with ginger, garlic, pepper, turmeric, and salt. Marinate 30 minutes.

2. While chicken is marinating, make barbecue sauce, mixing ketchup, Worcestershire sauce, dry mustard, jaggery or brown sugar, and vinegar. Add cayenne if desired. (Adjust seasonings to taste.) Pre-heat oven to 375.

3. Mix chicken with barbecue sauce, coating thoroughly. Cover with foil and bake 1 hour. (An instant-read thermometer near the bone should read 165°.)

4. Remove chicken to serving dish. Whisk liquid left in pan to make a nice sauce, drizzle over chicken, and serve with rice or roti.

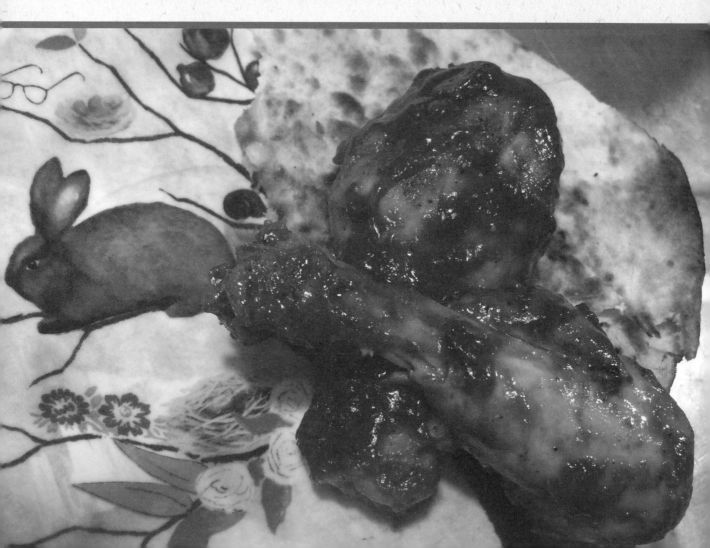

Fried Liver Curry / Eeral Kari

(30 minutes, serves 4)

I cook liver curry whenever I feel depleted. It is rich and full of iron, vitamin A, and protein, and can be very helpful to invalids building their health back up. There's a reason moms across the world tell kids to eat their liver—it's good for you! It's also delicious.

I also like to add chicken liver to a regular chicken curry—if doing that, just slice the liver and add it near the end of cooking, so it simmers for about fifteen minutes, picking up the curry seasonings. It will add a rich flavor and texture to the curry.

Note for vegetarians: Liver has a texture very close to seitan, and you can substitute seitan directly into this recipe. Firm tofu works too, though it doesn't pick up the seasonings as well.

1 lb. liver, sliced (from chicken or beef, or other substitutions as noted above)
1 medium onion, sliced
1 tsp. black mustard seed
1 tsp. cumin seeds
1 dozen curry leaves
2 tsp. oil
1 tsp. Sri Lankan curry powder
¼ tsp. ginger powder

¼ tsp. garlic powder
1 tsp. ground black pepper
1 tsp. salt
½ - 1 tsp. lime juice

1. Heat oil in a frying pan and add onion, mustard seeds, cumin, and curry leaves; fry on medium, stirring as needed, until golden.

2. While onions are cooking, mix spices with a little water or milk to make a thin paste.

3. Coat the liver with the spice mix (stirring gently in a bowl), and add to the onions, stirring to combine. (Be especially gentle stirring chicken liver, as it breaks apart easily.)

4. Cook, stirring, over medium heat, until it's nicely browned on the outside and still rosy on the inside. Add lime juice and stir gently for a few minutes until liquid is reduced. Serve with rice or bread; I particularly like it on toast.

Black Pork Curry / Panri
Iraichchi Kari / Padre Kari

(1 ½ hours, serves 6-8)

This traditional tangy, peppery dish gets its dark color from the combination of dark roasted curry powder, tamarind paste, and lots of ground black pepper. (The colloquial name 'padre kari' refers to the black robes of a padre / priest.) Tamarind paste is fairly easy to find in Mexican and Indian markets, or you can order it online. It keeps well in the pantry for a long time, even after opening. Typically, you'd leave a good portion of the fat on the pork pieces; it soaks up a ton of flavor, and is truly delectable, balancing the meat, which can otherwise be a bit dry after long cooking. But you can trim all the fat off if you'd prefer.

3 medium onions, chopped fine
2 Tbsp. ginger, chopped fine
4-5 cloves garlic , sliced
6-12 curry leaves (optional)
1 tsp. black mustard seed
1 tsp. cumin seed
3 Tbsp. vegetable oil
1 Tbsp. Sri Lankan curry powder
1 heaping tsp. salt
4 tsp. ground black pepper
3 lbs. pork shoulder, cubed, about 1-inch pieces, with some fat left on
3 tsp. tamarind paste
½ cup white vinegar

1. In a large pot, sauté onions, ginger, garlic, mustard seeds, cumin seeds, and curry leaves in oil on medium until onions are golden / translucent (not brown), stirring as needed.

2. Add curry powder, salt, pepper, stirring to combine, then turn heat to high. Add pork and sear, stirring occasionally, for a few minutes, to bring out the flavor of the meat.

3. Add tamarind paste and white vinegar; stir well, turn heat to medium, and cover. Cook one hour, stirring occasionally. Serve hot, with rice or bread.

Meatball Curry / Frikkadel

(1 hour, serves 8)

Frikkadels are a traditional European dish of meatballs prepared with ground meat, onion, bread, milk, eggs, and spices. They're popular in Afrikaner cuisine, and came to Sri Lanka with the Dutch colonization (1640 - 1796), but of course, developed their own unique character in Sri Lanka. You can make just the mild seasoned meatballs (in which case you'd make them on the smaller side, dip them in egg and breadcrumbs and deep fry them), or you can envelop them in a spicy curry sauce. Either way is yummy.

Meatballs:

> 1 Tbsp. butter
> 1 small onion, minced
> 1 Tbsp. ginger, minced
> 1 Tbsp. garlic, minced
> 2 lbs. of lean ground meat
> *Note: I recommend a mix of pork and beef, but you can also use lamb, goat, chicken, or turkey.*
> 2 tsp. paprika
> ¼ tsp. ground cinnamon
> ¼ tsp. ground cloves
> 1 ½ tsp. salt
> 1 tsp. ground black pepper

2 tsp. Worcestershire sauce
1 egg, beaten
3 slices of bread, torn into small pieces
½ cup milk
2-3 Tbsp. oil

Curry sauce:
2-3 Tbsp. oil
1 large onion, chopped
2 Tbsp. ginger, minced
3 cloves garlic, sliced
1-2 dozen curry leaves
3 green chilies, sliced
1 1-inch cinnamon stick
3 cloves
3 cardamom pods
1 Tbsp. cayenne
1 Tbsp. Sri Lankan curry powder
3 large tomatoes, chopped (or one 15 oz. can of diced tomatoes)
¼ cup vinegar
1 tsp. salt
1 cup coconut milk

1. Sauté onions, ginger, and garlic in butter in a large frying pan until golden.

2. Mix with ground meat, spices, Worcestershire sauce, and egg. Soak bread in milk to soften it, and mix in to the meatball mixture, which will be quite moist. (Traditionally, these are delicate, moist versions of meatballs, but if you prefer them more dry, you can add breadcrumbs as desired.)

3. Form into balls. (If you just want meatballs and not curry, after forming into balls, dip in beaten egg, roll in breadcrumbs, and then deep fry in a larger

quantity of oil.) Shallow fry in a little oil, just enough to brown the outside (they don't need to be cooked through). Stir very gently, as they break up easily. Remove to a plate (or two) and set aside.

4. Sauté onions, ginger, garlic, curry leaves, chilies, cinnamon, cloves, and cardamom in oil until onions are golden.

5. Add cayenne, cook for thirty seconds or so, stirring, then add curry powder, tomatoes, vinegar, and salt. Stir until well mixed, taste for seasoning and adjust as desired.

6. Add coconut milk and meatballs, stirring gently to mix well. Turn heat to medium and simmer 15 minutes, until meatballs are cooked through and flavors are well blended, stirring (gently) occasionally. Serve hot, with rice or bread.

Goat (Mutton) Curry / Aattu Iraichchi Kari

(45 minutes + marinating time, serves 4)

Most Sri Lankans (and others, particularly in India, Pakistan, Nepal, and Bangladesh) call goat 'mutton,' which can be confusing for those who expect sheep. But regardless of what you call it, goat on the bone makes a succulent curry; eating it with your hands makes it easy to suck out the delicious marrow. Goat is very popular in Sri Lanka, offering meat that is savory and less sweet than beef, but slightly more sweet than lamb.

2 lbs. goat, preferably chump chops with bones
1 Tbsp. Sri Lankan curry powder
⅓ cup ketchup
¼ cup Worcestershire sauce
1 tsp. salt
2 cups coconut milk, divided
3 medium onions, chopped fine
2 Tbsp. ginger, chopped fine
4-5 cloves garlic, sliced
8-12 curry leaves
1 2-inch cinnamon stick
3 Tbsp. vegetable oil
1 tsp. black mustard seed

1 tsp. cumin seed
1-2 Tbsp. cayenne
2-3 Tbsp. lime juice

1. Trim away any excess of fat (but leave some on for flavor), and chop goat into pieces with the bone in. Combine with curry powder, ketchup, Worcestershire sauce, salt, and 1 cup coconut milk in a large bowl to marinate, about 30-60 minutes.

2. In a large pot, sauté onions, ginger, and garlic in oil on medium-high with curry leaves, cinnamon stick, mustard seed, and cumin seeds until onions are golden / translucent (not brown), stirring as needed. Add cayenne and cook 1 minute, stirring.

3. Immediately add goat mixture to the pan, cover with remaining coconut milk and water to cover, and bring to a boil. Reduce heat to medium low and simmer for about 30 minutes, until the meat is tender and the gravy thickens. Add lime juice, season to taste, and serve hot with rice or bread.

Lamb Curry / Semmari Aattu Iraichchi Kari

(1 hour 15 minutes, serves 4)

This is a fairly mild preparation; you can add 1-2 teaspoons of cayenne if desired, while frying the onions. Creamy and succulent.

2 lbs. lamb shanks, cut off the bone into small pieces, bones reserved
1 Tbsp. Sri Lankan curry powder
1 tsp. ground turmeric
1 tsp. black pepper
1 tsp. salt
½ cup vinegar
3 medium onions, chopped fine
3 Tbsp. vegetable oil
1 tsp. black mustard seed
1 tsp. cumin seed
2 Tbsp. ginger, chopped fine
3-6 cloves garlic , crushed
4-5 green chilies, chopped
8-12 curry leaves
1 2-inch cinnamon stick
3 cardamom pods
3 cloves

1 cup water
2 cups coconut milk
½ cup chopped cilantro (optional)

1. In a bowl, combine lamb (pieces and bone) with curry powder, turmeric, black pepper, salt, and vinegar; set aside.

2. In a large pot, sauté onions, ginger, and garlic in oil on medium-high with remaining spices until onions are golden / translucent (not brown), stirring as needed.

3. Add the marinated lamb pieces and bone to the pot (reserving liquid) and fry about 5 minutes, browning the meat.

4. Add water to liquid in bowl and then add both to pot; add coconut milk as well. Bring to a boil, stirring. Cover, turn down heat to medium, and cook another 45 minutes, until lamb is well cooked.

5. Remove lid and simmer uncovered 15 minutes, until you have a rich gravy. Season to taste, garnish with coriander, and serve hot with rice or bread.

Beef Smoore / Mas Ismoru

(2-4 hours marinating, + 2 hours, serves 8)

This is a dish of Dutch / Sri Lankan origin, perfect for a Sunday roast, when you have time for long, slow (yet easy) cooking. Yummy with rice—also great in weekday lunch sandwiches on hearty Italian bread, or shredded into a folded roti, with some pickled onions and a little yogurt. Long-handled metal tongs will help with moving the large piece of hot meat. This is made to authentic Sri Lankan spice levels; reduce cayenne for a milder version. Delicious with a deep red wine; garnish with cilantro if desired. A fabulous dinner party dish.

3 lbs. chuck roast
3 Tbsp. ghee or vegetable oil
½ cup vinegar
1 Tbsp. salt
1 Tbsp. pepper
1 Tbsp. tamarind, dissolved in one cup water
2 medium onions, chopped fine
6 cloves garlic, chopped fine
1 Tbsp. fresh ginger, chopped fine
1 2-inch cinnamon stick
2 stalks curry leaves
1 stalk lemongrass, chopped
2 Tbsp. Sri Lankan curry powder

2 tsp. cayenne
1 tsp. ground turmeric
½ tsp. fenugreek seeds
2 tsp. salt
1 cup coconut milk

1. Pierce the beef all over with a
   fork or skewer and marinate in
   vinegar, 1 tablespoon salt, and 1
   tablespoon pepper for 2-4 hours.
   (I find this easiest to do in a
   plastic bag, turning periodically.)

2. Heat the oil or ghee on high in a
   large, heavy pot, and sear the beef
   until lightly brown on all sides, which will add great depth of flavor to the sauce.
   Remove the meat from the pan and set aside.

3. To the same pan, add the tamarind water, onions, garlic, ginger, cinnamon, curry
   leaves, lemongrass, curry powder, cayenne, turmeric, fenugreek, and remaining
   salt. Stir to combine, scraping up any browned meat on the bottom of the pan.

4. Return the meat to the pot, bring to a boil, cover the pot well (the steam needs to
   stay in, to cook the meat), and simmer gently until meat is tender, approximately
   2 hours.

5. Add coconut milk and simmer uncovered 15 minutes.

6. Remove meat to a serving dish; if the gravy is too thin, reduce it by boiling
   rapidly uncovered. Transfer gravy to a serving bowl. Slice the meat into the
   desired thickness, and pour gravy over the slices; serve hot with rice or bread.

Beef and Potato Curry

(1 hour, serves 6)

This was my favorite dish growing up, the one my mother always makes for me when I come home, and the first Sri Lankan dish I learned to cook, when I called home desperate from the dorms, begging her to teach me how to make it over the phone. It's also the first Sri Lankan dish my husband, Kevin, learned to cook—I came home once from a long plane flight, walked into the house, smelled the scent of this curry, that I hadn't even known he had learned how to make, and promptly burst into tears. Enjoy.

3-5 medium onions, chopped fine
2 Tbsp. ginger, chopped fine
4-5 cloves garlic , sliced
3 Tbsp. vegetable oil
1 tsp. black mustard seed
1 tsp. cumin seed
1-2 Tbsp. cayenne
3 lbs. chuck steak, cubed, about 1 inch pieces
⅓ cup ketchup
¼ cup Worcestershire sauce
1 Tbsp. Sri Lankan curry powder
1 heaping tsp. salt

3 pieces cinnamon stick

3 cloves

3 cardamom pods

1 dozen curry leaves

½ cup milk

3 medium russet potatoes, cut into large chunks

2-3 Tbsp. lime juice

1. In a large pot, sauté onions, ginger, and garlic in oil on medium-high with mustard seed and cumin seeds until onions are golden / translucent (not brown), stirring as needed. Add cayenne and cook 1 minute, stirring. Immediately stir in ketchup, Worcestershire sauce, curry powder, salt, cinnamon, cardamom, cloves, and curry leaves.

2. Add beef and stir on high for a minute or two, browning the meat. Add milk, stirring. Cover, turn down to medium, and let cook half an hour, stirring occasionally.

3. Add potatoes, stir well, and cover again. Cook until potatoes are cooked through, adding water if needed to maintain a nice thick sauce (and to keep food from burning), stirring occasionally. Add lime juice; stir until well blended. Serve hot with rice or bread.

Tangy Peppered Beef Stew

(2 hours, serves 8)

This is very similar to a traditional British beef stew, but the Sri Lankan version adds vinegar and peppercorns for a distinctly different flavor. I love to chew on the peppercorns for a bit of sharp bite, and will sometimes add *even more* peppercorns to the pot.

3 lbs. beef chuck, cubed, large pieces of fat removed
½ cup white wine
2 cups beef stock
2 Tbsp. ghee or vegetable oil
1 2-inch cinnamon stick
8 cloves
40 peppercorns
1 tsp. salt
2 cups vinegar
3 medium onions, peeled and cut in eighths
2-3 large potatoes, peeled and cut in large pieces
4 carrots, cut in large pieces
additional salt to taste

1. In a large stew pan, heat the oil on high, add the meat and brown on all sides (avoid crowding the pan, as that will cause it to steam instead of browning—do the meat in two batches if necessary).

2. When nicely browned, deglaze the pan with wine, stirring to scrape up browned bits. Add beef stock and a sufficient quantity of the water to cover the meat. Add the cinnamon, cloves, peppercorns, salt, and vinegar. Bring to a boil, then cover, turn down heat to low, and let simmer for 30 minutes.

3. Add the vegetables, turn the heat to high long enough for the stew to come to a boil, then turn it back down to low and continue to cook, uncovered, until the meat is tender and the vegetables are cooked through, about an hour. You're aiming for the sauce being reduced to a thick gravy, so add water or cook the liquid off as needed. Taste and add more salt if needed. Serve hot, with hearty white bread or rice.

FISH *and* SEAFOOD

Crab Curry, Jaffna-Style / Nandu Kari

Cuttlefish or Squid Curry / Kanavai Kari

Deviled Shrimp

Fish White Curry / Meen Kari

Mackerel and Egg Curry

Salmon Curry

Tamarind Shrimp Curry / Iral Kari

Spicy Fried Fish / Poricha Meen

Spicy-Tangy Fish / Ambulthiyal

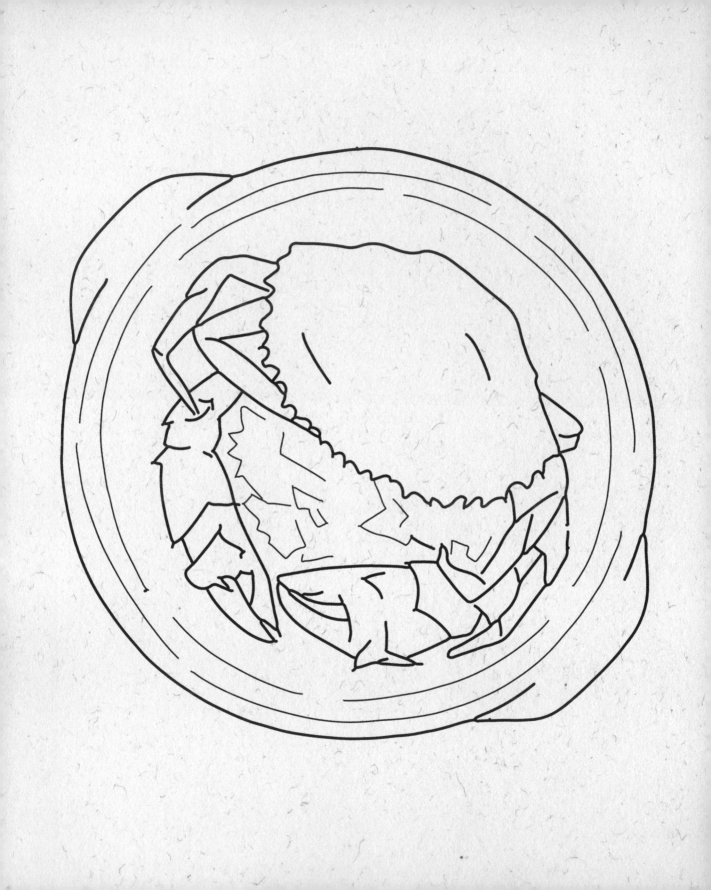

Crab Curry, Jaffna-Style / Nandu Kari

(90 minutes, serves 4-6)

A little effortful, this is classic dinner party food, brought out to impress your guests—at least the guests who are comfortable cracking the crab shells to extract the succulent curried meat. This is another dish that easiest to eat with your clean hands. If you visit Sri Lanka, this is one dish you should definitely try—it's a can't-miss specialty of the island! It's traditional to stir in murunga (drumstick) leaves at the end, but we weren't able to easily get them in Connecticut in the 1970s, and I promise you that my mother's crab curry was known far and wide nonetheless. They can now be found online, though, if you're aiming for full authenticity.

2 large crabs (about 4 lbs.)
1 onion, chopped fine
4 Tbsp. vegetable oil, divided 2 and 2
½ rounded tsp. fenugreek seeds
½ tsp. cumin seed
½ tsp. black mustard seed
2 Tbsp. Sri Lankan curry powder
1 cup ketchup
6 cloves garlic, chopped fine (optional)
1 2-inch cinnamon stick
1 Tbsp. salt

1 tsp. tamarind paste
4 cups thin coconut milk (2 cups coconut milk + 2 cups water)
10 curry leaves
2 cups coconut milk
1 sprig murunga (drumstick) leaves (optional)
1-3 Tbsp. lime juice

1. Remove large shells of crabs and discard fibrous tissue found under the shell. Divide each crab into 4 portions, breaking each body in half and separating large claws from body. You can cut large pieces into smaller segments. If you want, you can also cut pieces open with kitchen shears, to make eating easier, but leave the meat inside the shell.

2. In a large pan (large enough to hold the crab pieces in a single layer, ideally), fry onions in 2 tablespoons oil on low, stirring, until golden. Remove from pan and set aside.

3. Add remaining 2 tablespoons oil to pan, then add cumin, mustard, and fenugreek and cook on high for a few minutes, , stirring. Then add curry powder and stir to combine, add ketchup and stir to combine, and finally add 4 cups thin coconut

milk, cinnamon, salt, and tamarind. (Optional: add garlic if desired.) Mix well, bring to a boil, then cover and let simmer 20 minutes.

4. Add crabs and cook for 20 minutes if using raw crabs; try to keep the crabs submerged; cook in batches if necessary.

5. Add fried onions, curry leaves, and remaining coconut milk. Bring to a boil, then simmer, covered, 20-30 minutes. Add lime juice to taste, and stir in murunga leaves if using. Serve hot.

Cuttlefish or Squid Curry / Kanavai Kari

(90 minutes, serves 4-6)

Many Americans aren't used to eating squid, or if so, only as fried calamari. But squid makes a rich, flavorful curry that was always a hit at my mom's dinner parties.

1 lb. cuttlefish or squid
2 tsp. ghee or vegetable oil
3 small onions, chopped fine
1 stalk curry leaves
1 2-inch cinnamon stick
3 green chilies, chopped
3 cloves garlic, chopped
1 Tbsp. ginger, peeled and minced
¼ tsp. cayenne
¼ tsp. ground turmeric
1 heaping tsp. Sri Lankan curry powder
1 cup tomatoes, chopped
1 tsp. salt
2 cups coconut milk

1. Clean and wash the cuttlefish / squid; slice the bodies into rings.

2. Heat the oil in a pot and sauté the onions, curry leaves, cinnamon, green chilies, garlic, and ginger on medium-high, stirring as needed, until onions are golden-translucent.

3. Add the cayenne, turmeric, and curry powder; cook a few minutes more, stirring.

4. Add the tomatoes, salt, coconut milk, and cuttlefish, stirring to combine. Bring to a boil, then cover and turn down to medium. Cook 30-60 minutes, until cuttlefish are tender. Serve hot with rice.

Deviled Shrimp

(1 hour, serves 8-10)

ike all deviled dishes, this one is meant to be spicy. Great with rice and vegetables, but I also love to just eat this straight up on toast.

    3-5 medium onions, diced
    3 Tbsp. vegetable oil
    1 tsp. black mustard seed
    1 tsp. cumin seed
    1-2 Tbsp. cayenne
    2 lbs. shrimp, peeled and deveined
    ⅔ cup ketchup
    ⅓ cup soy sauce
    ⅓ cup Worcestershire sauce
    2 Tbsp. garlic, minced
    2 Tbsp. ginger, minced
    1 tsp. garlic powder
    1 tsp. ginger powder

1. In a large frying pan, sauté onions in oil on medium-high with mustard seed and cumin seed, until onions are half-cooked (about half as long as usual for a curry; you want them to retain their structure for this dish, rather than dissolve

into sauce). Add cayenne and cook one minute. Immediately add shrimp and remaining ingredients.

2. Cook a few minutes until shrimp is done. Sauce should be fairly thick—if it isn't, remove shrimp to a serving dish so it doesn't overcook, and then cook sauce down a little longer, then add to dish. Serve hot.

Fish White Curry / Meen Kari

(1 hour, serves 6)

This kind of delicate white milky curry was traditionally served to nursing mothers; fenugreek is a potent and effective galactagogue—'milk to bring the milk in,' as the old wives would say. Typically, one would leave out any pepper or chilies if cooking for that purpose, but if one is just cooking to enjoy, then black pepper, chili pepper, and green chilies may be added as desired.

2 T oil or ghee
2 lbs. firm white fish steaks or fillets (shark, seer fish, kingfish,
  swordfish, halibut, etc.)
1 tsp. ground turmeric
1-2 tsp. salt
1 tsp. black pepper or cayenne (optional)
juice of 1 lime (about 1-2 Tbsp.)
1-4 tsp. fenugreek
2 onions, finely sliced or diced
4 cloves garlic, sliced
3-6 green chilies, sliced (optional)
6-12 curry leaves
2 cups coconut milk

1. Wash fish and dry on paper towels. Cut into pieces if desired. Rub with turmeric, salt, pepper (if using), and lime juice; let marinate at least half an hour, so the

flesh tightens and firms—if you skip this step, the fish will flake apart while cooking.

2. Sauté fenugreek, onion, garlic, curry leaves, and green chilies (if using) in a large saucepan until onions are golden-translucent. Add coconut milk and bring to a boil, then turn heat down and simmer gently until onions are soft, about 10 minutes.

3. Add fish, turn up heat to high until just boiling, stirring constantly so the milk doesn't curdle, then turn back down and simmer an additional 10-15 minutes, stirring occasionally. Taste and adjust seasonings as desired. Serve with rice or stringhoppers and an assortment of sambols.

Note: Cubed potatoes would be a fine addition to this; you can either sauté them in with the onions, or add them with the coconut milk; you can parboil them first to be sure they cook through.

Mackerel and Egg Curry

(40 minutes, serves 4-6)

People get scared of this dish because they think mackerel is overly fishy—and food snobs may put their noses in the air when they realize I'm using canned fish. All I can say in response is that this is one of my all-time favorite dishes. When served with uppuma, it's complete comfort food, but it's also good with rice or bread, and it reheats well for several meals of yummy goodness. It's also cheap, while still packed full of healthy protein and fish oil—I practically lived on this in grad school.

3 medium onions, chopped

3 Tbsp. vegetable oil

1 tsp. black mustard seed

1 tsp. cumin seed

2 Tbsp. (less or more to taste) cayenne

1 Tbsp. Sri Lankan curry powder

⅓ cup ketchup

1 heaping tsp. salt

1-2 cups water

1 flat tsp. tamarind paste (or more to taste)

1 15 oz. can mackerel, drained and rinsed

4 hard-boiled eggs, peeled and sliced in half

1. Sauté onions in oil on high with mustard seed and cumin seeds until onions are golden / translucent (not brown). Add cayenne and cook 1 minute. Immediately add curry powder, ketchup, and salt. Stir well.

2. Add water and bring to a boil. Add tamarind paste and dissolve. Lower heat to medium and add mackerel. Cover and cook, stirring occasionally (and carefully, so as to not break up the fish too much). Cook until sauce thickens, 20-30 minutes. Add eggs gently to dish and spoon sauce over. Serve hot.

Salmon Curry

(45 minutes, serves 6)

2 lbs. salmon
¼ cup vegetable oil
3 onions, chopped
1 Tbsp. black mustard seed
1 Tbsp. cumin seed
1 tsp. fenugreek / methi seed
1 tsp. fennel seeds
6-12 curry leaves
1 tsp. salt
½ tsp. cayenne
1 tsp. Sri Lankan curry powder
2 cups coconut milk
juice of 1 lime (about 1-2 Tbsp.)

1. Wash fish and dry on paper towels. Cut into roughly 1 inch pieces.

2. Sauté onions on medium-high with seeds, curry leaves, and salt until golden-translucent, stirring as needed.

3. Add cayenne, curry powder, and coconut milk. Simmer for about 5-10 minutes, until well blended. Add lime juice, stirring so it doesn't curdle.

4. Add salmon and simmer an additional 10-15 minutes, until fish is cooked through, stirring occasionally. Taste and adjust seasonings as desired. Serve with rice or stringhoppers and an assortment of sambols.

Tamarind Shrimp Curry /
Iral Kari

(45 minutes, serves 4-6)

picy, tangy, dark, and savory. A great dinner party dish, and if you're cooking for a big party, this one can be easily made ahead and frozen; it reheats very well.

1 lb. raw shrimp, shelled (and shells reserved)
2 cups water
3 medium onions, chopped
3 Tbsp. vegetable oil
1 tsp. black mustard seed
1 tsp. cumin seed
2 Tbsp. (or more to taste) cayenne
1 Tbsp. Sri Lankan curry powder
⅓ cup ketchup
1 heaping tsp. salt
1 rounded tsp. tamarind paste

1. Boil shrimp shells in water 15 minutes or so. Drain, reserving flavorful water. Discard shells.

2. Sauté onions in oil on high with mustard seed and cumin seeds until onions are golden / translucent (not brown). Add cayenne and cook 1 minute. Immediately add curry powder, ketchup, and salt. Stir well.

3. Add reserved shrimp water and bring to a boil. Add tamarind paste and dissolve.

4. Lower heat to medium. Cover and cook, stirring occasionally, until sauce thickens, 20-30 minutes. When sauce is thick and well-reduced, add shrimp and cook until shrimp are firm and pink. Serve hot with rice or bread.

Spicy Fried Fish / Poricha Meen

(20 minutes, serves 4)

This is a quick, delicious dish, lovely with rice and a vegetable curry. You can take the skins off if you want, but honestly, they are the tastiest part. Since we eat with our hands, it's relatively easy to eat around the bones, so we wouldn't typically remove the bones before frying, but you certainly can if you want to.

> 2 lbs. fish steaks, cut into pieces; kingfish, mackerel, and shark are
>   traditional, but salmon also works well
> ½ tsp. ground turmeric
> 2 Tbsp. lime juice
> 2 tsp. cayenne
> 1-2 tsp. salt
> oil for shallow-frying

1. Mix fish pieces with turmeric, lime juice, cayenne, and salt in a bowl; let marinate fifteen minutes.

2. Heat oil; once it is hot, add the fish pieces. Fry for a few minutes on one side, then flip them over and cook for a few minutes on the other side. Serve hot.

Spicy-Tangy Fish / Ambulthiyal

(30 minutes, serves 4)

Ambulthiyal comes from the southwestern coastal town of Ambalangoda, and traditionally would have been made in a clay pot. It is popular throughout the south of Sri Lanka, a dry and spicy preparation originally used to preserve fish. It is also served with kiri bath (traditional Sinhalese milk rice) for New Year's. Ambulthiyal is intensely flavored—a little goes a long way! This recipe is done to authentic spice levels; you can cut back the cayenne if desired. It's the only Sinhalese dish in the cookbook; my friend Samanthi made it so delectably, I just had to learn how to make it.

1 Tbsp. tamarind paste dissolved in 4 Tbsp. water
1 lb. tuna, swordfish, or other firm fish
juice of 1 lime (about 1-2 Tbsp.)
4 tsp. cayenne
1 tsp. ground black pepper
1 tsp. salt
½ cup water
6 cloves
1 Tbsp. ginger, sliced
5 cloves of garlic, sliced or mashed
1 dozen curry leaves

1. Cut the fish into large pieces and rinse them with the lime juice (which will lessen fishy smell and firm the fish up). Arrange the pieces in a single layer in a frying pan.

2. Blend the tamarind water, cayenne, pepper, and salt. Mix with the fish in the pan, coating each piece thoroughly.

3. Add the cloves, ginger, garlic, curry leaves, and water, and bring to a boil.

4. Simmer until all the gravy has been reduced and the fish pieces are quite dry, about fifteen minutes. Serve hot with rice and curries, or pack with bread for a picnic food.

VEGETABLES

CURRY

(vegetables cooked in coconut milk)

Beet Curry

Carrot Curry

Cashew Curry / Kaju Kari

Drumstick Curry / Murungakkai Kari

Eggplant Curry / Kaththarikkai Kari

Green Mango Curry / Maankai Kari

Green Jackfruit Curry / Palakkai Kari

Okra Curry / Vendikkai Kari

Ripe Jackfruit Curry / Palapazham Kari

DEVILED

(vegetables fried with cayenne, tomato, and onions)

Deviled Potatoes / Urulai Kizhangu

PORIYAL
(vegetables fried with seasoned onions)

Asparagus Poriyal

Brussels Sprouts Poriyal

Cauliflower Poriyal

Eggplant, Potato, and Pea Pod Poriyal

Mixed Vegetable Poriyal

TEMPERED
(cooked vegetables mixed with seasoned onions)

Tempered Lentils / Paruppu

Tempered Potatoes

VARAI
(steamed or stir-fried vegetables with coconut)

Broccoli Varai

Cabbage Varai / Muttaikoss Varai

Green Bean Varai

SPECIAL PREPARATIONS

Lime-Masala Mushrooms

Vegetable and Lentil Stew / Sambar

BASIC
APPROACHES
to VEGETABLES

CURRY *(vegetables cooked in coconut milk):* This is a standard curry approach— sauté onions with spices, add vegetables and coconut milk, simmer until cooked.

DEVILED *(vegetables fried with cayenne, tomato, and onions):* Deviling is traditionally used for seafood, chicken, and meat, but deviled potatoes are delicious, and I would imagine that you could approach many other vegetables the same way.

PORIYAL *(vegetables sautéed with seasoned onions):* Poriyal is a Tamil dish consisting of sautéed and spiced shredded vegetables. Similar dishes appear in other parts of South Asia, under different names.

TEMPERED *(cooked vegetables mixed with seasoned onions):* I used to be really confused when my mom referred to 'tempered potatoes' or other tempered dishes. In Western cooking, 'tempering' means to slowly bring up the temperature of a cold or room temperature ingredient, by adding small amounts of a hot or boiling liquid. Adding the hot liquid gradually prevents the cool ingredient (such as eggs) from cooking or setting. In Western cooking, tempering typically refers to either chocolate or eggs.

In South Asian cuisine, tempering is a widely used cooking method; you heat spices in hot oil or ghee, and then add them to your dish at the end of cooking. The hot oil extracts the flavors of the spices and intensifies their effect. South Asian tempering is done either at the beginning of the cooking process or as a final flavoring at the end—or sometimes both! The ingredients are usually added in rapid succession, rarely together, with those requiring longer cooking added earlier and those requiring less cooking added later. For instance, you'd add black mustard seeds to the hot oil first and then later add chopped garlic, which could burn if added earlier.

You can use this method with a wide variety of spices, for a wide variety of vegetables; you can simply mix tempered onions with boiled potatoes, or add them to a simmered lentil curry. Tempering highlights flavors that have already cooked into the dish, adding a bright, fresh seasoning note.

VARAI *(steamed or stir-fried vegetables with coconut)·* A varai is a mixture of greens and coconut traditionally cooked in a dry skillet. Some recipes use a little oil, but generally, this is a light, healthy way to cook vegetables. In Sri Lanka, a varai is often made with the leaves of plants not found in American grocery stores, but it can be prepared with broccoli, cauliflower, collard greens, mustard greens, cabbage, etc.

The greens are often cooked without any oil, so the only fat comes from the coconut. I strongly recommend using fresh or frozen rather than dried coconut if possible (and definitely not sweetened), because the flavor and taste will be much better. But if dried is all you have, rehydrate it in a little heated coconut milk beforehand.

Often, a greens dish will be made as a fresh sambol first, for lunch, and then what remains will be turned into a varai, which will keep better, and may be eaten with dinner, or at breakfast the next morning.

Beet Curry

(30 minutes, serves 4)

This dish has a lovely sweet flavor with just a hint of spice—beets have a higher sugar content than any other vegetable. The lime tang beautifully balances the sweetness and the spice, for a flavor characteristic of Sri Lankan cuisine.

3 medium onions, chopped fine
3 Tbsp. vegetable oil
¼ tsp. black mustard seed
¼ tsp. cumin seed
4 large beets (about 1 lb.), peeled, cut in thick matchsticks
1-2 rounded tsp. salt
1 rounded tsp. ground turmeric
2-3 tsp. lime juice
1-3 chopped green chilies
2 dozen curry leaves, optional
2 cups coconut milk

1. Sauté onions in oil on high with mustard seed and cumin seeds until onions are golden / translucent (not brown). Add beets, salt, turmeric, lime juice, chilies, and curry leaves. Continue cooking on high about 10-15 minutes, stirring occasionally, just enough so onions and beets don't burn—you want that beautifully caramelized flavor coming through.

2. Lower heat to medium and add coconut milk. Cook, stirring frequently, until beets are cooked through and coconut milk has reduced to simply coating the beets, about 10 minutes. Serve hot.

Carrot Curry

(20 minutes, serves 4)

This carrot curry is a lovely dish for early spring, and is the perfect accompaniment for beef curry. For a variation, you can switch out half the carrots for green beans, which brings a pleasant contrast and some extra nutrition to your plate.

> 3 medium onions, chopped
> 3 Tbsp. vegetable oil
> ¼ tsp. black mustard seed
> ¼ tsp. cumin seed
> 6 large carrots, peeled and cut into coins
> 1 rounded tsp. salt
> 1 rounded tsp. ground turmeric
> ½ - 1 cup coconut milk

1. Sauté onions in oil on high with mustard seed and cumin seeds until onions are golden. Add carrots, turmeric, and salt. Cook on medium-high, stirring, until carrots are mostly cooked, about 10 minutes.

2. Add coconut milk and turn heat down to low; simmer until the sauce thickens, stirring frequently, about 3-5 more minutes. Be careful not to curdle the milk by cooking on high heat. Serve hot.

Cashew Curry / Kaju Kari

(1 hour, serves 4-6)

Cashews are relatively expensive, compared to most vegetables; this is a luscious dish served to vegetarian dinner guests, unctuous and rich.

> 3 medium onions, diced
> 3 Tbsp. vegetable oil
> ¼ tsp. black mustard seed
> ¼ tsp. cumin seed
> 8-12 curry leaves
> 1 2-inch cinnamon stick
> 1 Tbsp. Sri Lankan curry powder
> 1 lb. roasted, salted cashews
> 1 can coconut milk
> 1 Tbsp. lime juice
> salt to taste (about ½ - 1 tsp.)

1. In a large pot, sauté onions in oil on medium-high with mustard seed, cumin seed, curry leaves, and cinnamon stick, until onions are golden / translucent (not brown). Add curry powder, cashews, and coconut milk.

2. Lower heat to medium. Cover and cook, stirring periodically, until cashews are soft and sauce is thick, about 30 minutes. Remove cover, taste, and add salt if desired. Add lime juice; simmer a few additional minutes, stirring. Serve hot.

Note: Traditionally, you'd start with raw whole cashews and soak them for two hours before cooking, which makes for a more tender finished product. I'm perfectly happy with the results from roasted, salted cashews.

Drumstick Curry / Murungakkai Kari

(1 hour, serves 4-6)

Drumsticks (moringa oleifera) are extremely popular vegetables in Sri Lanka and South Asia, and are reputed to have many health benefits. They're commonly prepared for women during and after pregnancy, and are said to help heal wounds and ease the discomfort of childbirth; midwives claim they help with post-partum depression as well. More than one account I read called it 'meat for vegetarians,' and the preparation below is cooked in a similar way to my beef curry, using dark roasted curry powder, though drumsticks are also commonly cooked in a mild yellow curry preparation.

Drumsticks are a vegetable that I've been unable so far to find fresh in Chicagoland, so I make this from frozen; you can also use canned. This would be tricky to eat with knife and fork, because you really need to scrape the flesh of the vegetable off the tough, fibrous exterior stalk with your teeth, so I recommend eating these with your hand, served with rice. Alternatively, you can chew them to get out all the flavor, and then discard the fibrous remains.

I recommend serving drumsticks with lentils, chickpeas, or something else fairly substantial, as there's not a lot of 'meat' for the bulk of the dish. Plenty of deliciousness, though!

1 lb. frozen drumsticks (or 4 long fresh drumsticks, cut to
  roughly 3-inch pieces)
¼ cup oil
2 medium onions, chopped
1 tsp. fenugreek seeds
1 stalk curry leaves
2 Tbsp. ginger, minced
6 cloves garlic , chopped
3 green chilies, sliced lengthwise
3 tsp. Sri Lankan curry powder
1 tsp. salt
2 cups water
1 cup coconut milk
½ tsp. tamarind paste

1. Heat oil in a large frying pan, and fry drumsticks for a few minutes, browning the exteriors; remove to a dish.

2. Add onions, fenugreek, curry leaves, ginger, garlic, and chilies to the oil, and sauté until onions are golden-brown.

3. Add drumsticks back to pan, with curry powder, salt, and water; cover and cook until drumsticks are tender, about twenty minutes.

4. Stir in coconut milk and tamarind, and simmer for a few more minutes, until well blended. Serve hot with rice.

Eggplant Curry / Kaththarikkai Kari

(30 minutes draining time + 30 minutes, serves 6)

y mother's eggplant curry was always a huge hit at Sri Lankan dinner parties, and is particularly popular with vegetarians.

1 lb. eggplant, roughly 1-inch cubes
1 tsp. ground turmeric
1 tsp. salt
2 onions, chopped coarsely
½ cup oil or ghee
1 tsp. cumin seed
1 tsp. black mustard seed
1 dozen curry leaves
1 tsp. brown sugar
1 tsp. Sri Lankan curry powder
½ cup coconut milk

1. Prep eggplant—rub with turmeric and salt and then set in a colander to drain at least 30 minutes, which will draw out the bitter water. Blot dry with paper towels.

2. Sauté onions in oil on medium-high, stirring, with cumin seed, black mustard seed, and curry leaves, until golden.

3. Add eggplant, sugar, and curry powder, and sauté for another ten minutes or so, until eggplant is nicely fried. (Add more oil or ghee if needed.)

4. Add coconut milk and simmer for a few minutes until well blended. Serve hot with rice or roti—particularly nice for a vegetarian dinner with lentils as the main protein.

Variation: Eggplant and bell pepper work well together in this dish; just add chopped bell pepper about five minutes into frying the eggplant for a nice sweet element to the dish. Sometimes I make a nightshade curry, adding potatoes and tomatoes as well—small cubed potatoes would go into the onions first, then eggplant and spices, then bell pepper, then tomato, with a few minutes between each addition.

Green Mango Curry /
Maankai Kari

(30 minutes, serves 6)

his dish can be traced as far back as the fifth century, when it was served at the court of King Kasyapa of Sigiriya (famed for his luxurious Sky Palace).

1 Tbsp. ghee or vegetable oil
3 small onions, minced
3 cloves garlic, chopped
1 Tbsp. ginger, chopped
3 tsp. black mustard seed
2 stalks curry leaves
3 green chilics, chopped
3 Tbsp. vinegar
3 tsp. Sri Lankan curry powder
1 tsp. cinnamon
1 tsp. salt
3 large green mangoes, peeled and cut into long, thick pieces
1 can coconut milk
½ cup water
1 Tbsp. sugar

1. Heat the oil in a pan and sauté the onion, garlic, ginger, mustard seeds, curry leaves, and chilies until the onions are soft.

2. Add the vinegar, curry powder, cinnamon, salt, and half a can of coconut milk with ½ cup water—stir to combine.

3. Add the mango slices, bring to a boil, and simmer until the mango is just tender, about ten minutes.

4. Add the rest of the coconut milk and sugar to the curry; bring to a boil, reduce the heat, and simmer for about five minutes. The gravy should be thick enough to thoroughly coat the mango. Serve hot with rice or bread.

Green Jackfruit Curry / Palakkai Kari

(30 minutes, serves 6)

Young jackfruit has a texture similar to meat, though softer; it's more delicate, as is the flavor. It's easy to find online in cans, packed in brine; it's also often available at grocery stores, especially ones that cater to vegetarians. If you can find it frozen (often in Indian stores), that will hold up very nicely to cooking, and be much less labor-intensive than working with fresh. This savory curry sauce is identical to what I'd use for beef, but gives a notably different (and delicious) result when cooked with jackfruit instead. I'd serve this with rice, a green vegetable, and chutneys, pickles, and/or sambols.

Note: For details about how to use ripe *jackfruit, see the Ripe Jackfruit Curry recipe.*

2 medium onions, chopped fine
1 Tbsp. ginger, chopped fine
3 cloves garlic , chopped fine
3 Tbsp. vegetable oil
¼ tsp. black mustard seed
¼ tsp. cumin seed
1 Tbsp. cayenne
1 tsp. Sri Lankan curry powder
1 lb. young jackfruit, cut into bite-size pieces

⅓ cup ketchup
¼ cup Worcestershire sauce (optional)
1 tsp. salt
2 Tbsp. lime juice
1 cup coconut milk + 1 cup water

1. In a large pot, sauté onions, ginger, and garlic in oil on medium-high with mustard seed and cumin seeds until onions are golden / translucent (not brown), stirring as needed. Add cayenne and cook 1 minute, stirring. Immediately stir in curry powder, ketchup, Worcestershire sauce, salt, and lime juice.

2. Add jackfruit and stir on high for a few minutes. Add coconut milk and water, stirring gently to combine. Turn down to medium, and let cook 15-20 minutes, stirring occasionally; add water if needed. Serve hot with rice or bread.

Okra Curry / Vendikkai Kari

(45 minutes, serves 6)

For those afraid of okra, I promise you that this will not be slimy at all. A tender vegetable dish, with a nice toothsome chew to it.

Note: This recipe is a little fussy, because it's designed to make sure the okra is quite dry before cooking—alternatively, you could skip step 2, and add the okra at the end of step 3, before adding curry powder and coconut milk. That would involve just one pan, so easier and faster—about thirty minutes total.

1 lb. okra, washed and dried
½ tsp. ground turmeric
½ tsp. salt
vegetable oil for frying
2 Tbsp. ghee or vegetable oil
1 onion, sliced thin
3 cloves garlic, chopped
½ tsp. black mustard seed
½ tsp. cumin seed
½ tsp. fenugreek seed
3-4 dried red chili pods, crumbled
½ tsp. Sri Lankan curry powder
½ can coconut milk

1. Slice okra thinly on the diagonal, and mix with turmeric and salt.

2. Heat oil in a small frying pan, to deep-fry okra in batches, removing to drain on paper towels. (At this point, okra may be served as is, for a yummy snack.)

3. In a small saucepan, heat ghee or oil and sauté onion, garlic, mustard, cumin, fenugreek, and chili pods until onions are soft and golden.

4. Add curry powder and coconut milk; simmer for a few minutes, stirring, until well blended.

5. Add okra to the pot and stir for a few minutes more on low, until well blended. Serve hot with rice.

Ripe Jackfruit Curry /
Palapazham Kari

(1 ½ hours, serves 6)

Jackfruit is enjoying a surge of popularity in the West recently, making it somewhat easier to find fresh jackfruit than previously, though you still may need to venture to an Asian grocery store. You may also be able to find frozen sections there. Do not use canned jackfruit in syrup, as it will be much too sweet.

The trickiest part of this dish is removing the jackfruit pulp from the seeds, fibers, and husk—jackfruit is a little sticky, and oiling your hands beforehand will help. The internet offers many videos showing the process of removing the fruit, which is fairly simple in the end—cut it open, cut out the inedible core, and then separate out the firm fruit, which is similar in appearance to mango, but is more fibrous, and therefore holds up to long cooking.

Once the fruit has been extracted and chopped, and the onions and tomatoes chopped as well, this is an extremely simple one-pot dish, sweet and subtle.

> 1 lb. fresh ripe jackfruit (yellow fruit), chopped small
> 1 cup thick coconut milk
> ½ cup water
> 2 small onions, minced
> 1 stalk curry leaves
> 1 tsp. ground turmeric
> 1 tsp. cayenne

½ tsp. Sri Lankan curry powder
1 cup tomatoes, chopped
1 Tbsp. tamarind paste
1 2-inch cinnamon stick
1 tsp. salt
juice of ½ a lime (about ½-1 Tbsp.)

1. Combine ingredients in a pot; stir to mix.

2. Bring to a boil, then cover, turn down heat, and simmer for about an hour, until the jackfruit is tender, stirring occasionally. Add water if needed to keep the sauce from burning.

3. Cook down until the fruit is coated in a thick curry sauce. Serve hot with rice and ideally a dry, spicy-salty protein, like fried fish or crispy chickpeas, for contrast.

Deviled Potatoes /
Urulai Kizhangu

(30 minutes, serves 4)

This was the first vegetable dish I learned to make, and I still find it addictive. It's great with rice and a meat curry, but also works quite well mashed up as a party spread with triangles of toasted naan or pita. For a little more protein, you could add canned and drained chickpeas when you add the potatoes.

> 3 medium onions, chopped
> 3 Tbsp. vegetable oil
> ¼ tsp. black mustard seed
> ¼ tsp. cumin seed
> 1-2 Tbsp. (or more to taste) cayenne
> 3 medium russet potatoes, cubed
> 3 Tbsp. ketchup
> 1 rounded tsp. salt
> ½ cup milk or coconut milk, optional

1. Sauté onions in oil on high with mustard seed and cumin seeds until onions are golden / translucent (not brown). Add cayenne and cook 1 minute. Immediately add potatoes, ketchup, and salt.

2. Lower heat to medium and add enough water so the potatoes don't burn (enough to cover usually works well). Cover and cook, stirring periodically, until potatoes are cooked through, about 20 minutes.

3. Remove lid and simmer off any excess water; the resulting curry sauce should be fairly thick, so that the potatoes are coated with sauce, rather than swimming in liquid. Add milk, if desired, to thicken sauce and mellow spice level; stir until well blended. Serve hot.

Asparagus Poriyal

(15 minutes, serves 4)

This particular recipe is entirely my own invention (though they do make asparagus poriyal in Sri Lanka frequently). I think it came out quite well! A lovely dish for a spring luncheon, with bright green asparagus contrasting beautifully with the chopped red tomato.

1 large onion, sliced
1 Tbsp. ginger, minced
3 cloves garlic, chopped
3 green chilies, chopped
1 dozen curry leaves (optional)
1 tsp. black mustard seed
1 tsp. cumin seed
½ tsp. fennel seed
½ tsp. cayenne
1 tsp. salt
¼ cup ghee or vegetable oil
1 lb. asparagus, tough ends removed, cut into pieces
1 Tbsp. lime juice
½ cup tomatoes, chopped

1. Sauté everything but the asparagus, lime juice, and tomatoes in oil or ghee until onions are transparent (not browned), about five minutes.

2. Add asparagus and lime juice and mix thoroughly; cover and cook five minutes.

3. Remove lid and check asparagus; it should be tender-crisp; sauté a bit more if needed. Stir in tomatoes; cook a few minutes more. Serve hot, with rice and curries.

Brussels Sprouts Poriyal

(20 minutes, serves 4-6)

I never used to like brussels sprouts, but I think it's just that I didn't really know them. Kevin convinced me to try them roasted with olive oil, salt, and pepper, and from there to this was not so far. Now I adore them.

Note: For a fancy appetizer, serve in little glass bowls with tiny forks; a pomegranate seed garnish is a delicious addition, and makes for a holiday festive look; chopped dried cranberries also work!

> 2 onions, chopped
> ¼ cup vegetable oil
> ½ thumb-sized piece of ginger, peeled and grated
> 3 cloves garlic, minced
> ½ tsp. cumin seed
> ½ tsp. black mustard seed
> 1 lb. brussels sprouts
> 1 tsp. salt
> ½ tsp. ground turmeric

1. Sauté onions, garlic, and ginger in oil with mustard seeds and cumin seeds until golden. (You can do this on medium, stirring occasionally, while doing the next step, but be careful not to burn them.)

2. Cut ends off brussels sprouts and cut larger pieces in half (or even quarters if they're really huge), so they're all approximately the same size.

3. Microwave sprouts three minutes (this cooks them partway so that they don't take so long on the stovetop that your onions start to burn).

4. Add sprouts to onion mixture, with turmeric and salt. Cook on medium-high, stirring occasionally, until cooked through, about ten minutes.

Cauliflower Poriyal

(25 minutes, serves 4)

The key to this dish is sautéing the cauliflower until it's browned—the browned bits will be the tastiest. I generally like to serve this dish with beef or pork curry; the slightly salty flavor complements those meats well. This is, oddly, one of my picky children's favorite dishes, and has often proved popular with my friends' children as well. I think it's all the frying.

> 3 medium onions, chopped coarsely
> 3 Tbsp. vegetable oil
> ¼ tsp. black mustard seed
> ¼ tsp. cumin seed
> 1 medium cauliflower, chopped into bite-size pieces
> 1 rounded tsp. salt
> 1 rounded tsp. ground turmeric

1. Sauté onions in oil on high in a large nonstick frying pan with mustard seed and cumin seed, until onions are slightly softened (not brown). Add cauliflower, turmeric, and salt. (I've made this in a regular frying pan, and found that it's difficult not to burn it; if you don't use non-stick, you'll need to stir constantly.)

2. Cook on medium-high, stirring frequently, until cauliflower is browned (mostly yellow, but with a fair bit of brown on the flatter parts). This takes a while—don't stop too early, or it won't be nearly as tasty. Serve hot.

Eggplant, Potato, and
Pea Pod Poriyal

(20 minutes, serves 4)

he lush flavor of the eggplant balances well with the soft potatoes and crisp sweetness of the pea pods.

2 Japanese eggplants (or one large globe eggplant), diced small
1 tsp. salt
1 tsp. ground turmeric
2 small onions, diced
½ cup oil or ghee
1 tsp. black mustard seed
1 tsp. cumin seed
1 dozen curry leaves
1 Tbsp. ginger, minced
3 cloves garlic, chopped
3 small russet potatoes (same volume as eggplant), peeled & diced small
3 green chilies, minced
1 cup pea pods
1 tsp. lime juice

1   Mix eggplant in a bowl with salt and turmeric, set aside.

2. Sauté onions in oil or ghee with mustard seed, cumin seed, curry leaves, ginger, and garlic until golden-translucent.

3. Add potatoes and green chilies, stir occasionally until mostly cooked, about ten minutes.

4. Drain liquid from eggplant (it will have given off some water) and blot dry with paper towels. Add eggplant to pan, mix well, and fry an additional 5-10 minutes.

5. While that's cooking, chop up some pea pods (green beans or sugar snap peas would also work well, or just frozen peas). Add to pan and sauté a few minutes more; stir in lime juice. Serve hot with rice or bread.

Mixed Vegetable Poriyal

(20 minutes, serves 4)

This one is super-convenient, since you can keep the frozen veggies in your freezer and it thus doesn't require going to the grocery store, as long as you already have onions. And if you don't already have onions, well, you're going to have trouble cooking these dishes, is all I can say. I've included two variations that work well, using fresh vegetables, but there are many other possibilities. This is one of the first dishes I learned to cook, and I made it often during grad school.

3 medium onions, chopped
3 Tbsp. vegetable oil
¼ tsp. black mustard seed
¼ tsp. cumin seed
1 large package frozen mixed vegetables, thawed and drained, bite-size pieces
1 rounded tsp. salt
1 rounded tsp. ground turmeric

1. Sauté onions in oil on high with mustard seed and cumin seeds until onions are golden / translucent (not brown). Add mixed vegetables, turmeric, and salt.

2. Cook on medium-high, stirring periodically, until vegetables are cooked through and almost dry. Serve hot with rice or bread.

Note: The variation below using fresh vegetables will take longer, since you need to add in prep time, and since potatoes take longer to cook.

Variation: Potatoes, Peas, and Tomatoes: In a large frying pan, sauté chopped onions in oil on high with mustard seed, cumin seeds, and curry leaves; cook until onions are golden / translucent. Add chopped and peeled russet potatoes, turmeric, and salt. Mix well.

Cook on medium-high, stirring occasionally, until potatoes are mostly cooked through and starting to stick. Add chopped tomatoes and continue to stir. When tomatoes are well-reduced, add peas and continue to stir. Cook until peas have lost their bright green color and much of their moisture; the ingredients should be well blended in flavor, and the potatoes should be somewhat browned. Serve hot with rice or bread.

Tempered Lentils / Paruppu

(1 hour, serves 6)

Lentils are a staple dish in Sri Lanka—across the country, people eat what we call paruppu daily, at breakfast, lunch, and dinner. It's terribly good for you, very affordable, and also delicious. I used to dislike lentils, or I thought I did, but it turned out I only disliked my mother's version (which everyone else loved, so I blame my being a slightly picky kid). I was converted to lentils through my adult discovery of Ethiopian food, a cuisine which cooks the lentils to a soft porridge-like consistency; now I am quite fond of them. This recipe is adapted from Charmaine Solomon's *The Complete Asian Cookbook.*

2 cups red lentils
1 can coconut milk, plus 1 can hot water
1 dried red chili, broken into pieces
a pinch of ground saffron
1 tsp. pounded Maldive fish (optional)
2 Tbsp. ghee or vegetable oil
2 medium onions, finely sliced
6 curry leaves
1 2-inch cinnamon stick
3 strips of lemon rind (about a quarter lemon)
salt to taste (about ¾ -1 tsp.)

1. Put lentils in a saucepan with the coconut milk, chili, and saffron (and Maldive fish, if using). (If you don't have red lentils, you can use a different variety, but it will notably change the flavor.) Fill the can with hot water and add that as well; this will ensure you don't waste any coconut yumminess. Bring to a boil, then cover and simmer until lentils are soft, about forty-five minutes. Stir periodically and add more water if needed; it's fine if the bottom starts to stick a little—just scrape it up.

2. In another saucepan, heat the oil and fry the onions, curry leaves, cinnamon, and lemon rind until onions are golden-brown.

3. Reserve half the onions for garnishing the dish and add the lentil mixture to the saucepan. Stir well, add salt to taste, and cook down until thick, like porridge. Serve with rice and curries.

Note: Some people like their paruppu more watery, but I think they're just wrong. Still, cook to your preference. I tend to leave the Maldive fish out, since I often make this dish when I'm cooking for vegetarians.

Tempered Potatoes

(20 minutes, serves 4)

For vegetarians, or those who don't like pungent dried fish, just leave the Maldive fish out (you may want a bit more salt to compensate).

3 russet potatoes, peeled
1 onion, sliced
3-4 cloves garlic , sliced
2-4 tsp. Maldive fish (optional)
3 Tbsp. lime juice
1-2 tsp. dried red chili pieces
½ tsp. cayenne
¼ tsp. ground turmeric
¼ cup vegetable oil
1 ½ tsp. black mustard seed
1 2-inch cinnamon stick
1 dozen curry leaves
1 tsp. salt

1. Boil potatoes, drain, and cut into large chunks or small dice, as you prefer.

2. In a medium bowl, mix these ingredients: onion, garlic, Maldive fish, lime juice, chili pieces, cayenne, turmeric, and salt.

3. Heat oil in a saucepan on medium heat; when oil is ready add mustard seeds and let it pop up (nearly 2-4 seconds). Then add cinnamon and curry leaves and let it fry for 1-2 minutes. Then add the onion mixture and stir to mix.

4. Turn heat to medium, and fry, stirring occasionally, until onions are translucent-golden, about 10 minutes; be careful not to burn them. The mixture should be very aromatic by this stage.

5. Add potatoes into the onion mixture, mixing well, but don't break the potatoes into small pieces. Stir for a minute or two until well blended; taste and add salt and/or lime juice as desired. Serve with rice or bread.

Broccoli Varai

(30 minutes, serves 4)

A good way to get green vegetables into children.

Note: I keep this fairly mild, so my kids will eat it, but for a spicier (and more traditional) version, chop 2-3 green chilies, and stir them in during step 1.

1 pound broccoli (crowns and/or stalks), chopped fine (by hand or in food processor)
1 medium onion, chopped fine
1-2 Tbsp. vegetable oil
6-12 curry leaves
1 1-inch cinnamon stick
¼ tsp. black mustard seed
¼ tsp. cumin seed
1 tsp. black pepper (or cayenne)
1 tsp. salt
½ tsp. ground turmeric
½ cup shredded unsweetened coconut
2 Tbsp. oil or butter (optional)
1 tsp. sugar (optional)
1-2 tsp. lime juice (optional)

1. Sauté onions in oil on high with curry leaves, cinnamon, mustard seeds, and cumin seeds until onions are golden / translucent (not brown).

2. Add broccoli, salt, pepper, and turmeric; fry, stirring, for a few minutes. (If the broccoli starts sticking to the bottom of the pan, you can add a little water.)

3. Add in coconut and stir for five minutes.

4. Taste, and stir in sugar and/or lime juice if desired. Serve hot, with rice and curries.

Cabbage Varai / Muttaikoss Varai

(15-20 minutes, serves 8)

Sweet, firm, rich with coconut.

> 8 oz. cabbage
> 1 medium onion, minced
> 2 fresh green chilies, seeded and chopped
> ¼ rounded tsp. ground turmeric
> ¼ rounded tsp. freshly ground black pepper
> 1 rounded tsp. salt
> ½ cup shredded unsweetened coconut

1. Shred cabbage finely. Wash well, drain, and put into a large saucepan. Don't worry about drying the water clinging to the cabbage—you actually want that water to help steam the cabbage.

2. Add all the other ingredients except the coconut. Cover and cook gently until cabbage is tender, stirring periodically.

3. Uncover, add coconut, stir well, and when the liquid in the pan has been absorbed by the coconut, remove from heat. Allow to cool before serving.

Green Bean Varai

(15-20 minutes, serves 8)

A fresh, green element on the dinner plate.

> 1 medium onion, minced
> 1 tsp. black mustard seed
> ¼ rounded tsp. ground turmeric
> 1-3 dried red chilies, broken into pieces (optional)
> 1 lb. green beans, chopped fine (in a food processor is fine)
> ¼ rounded tsp. freshly ground black pepper
> 1 rounded tsp. salt
> ½ cup shredded unsweetened coconut

1. Cook onions with turmeric, black mustard seed, and chilies in a dry pan over high heat, stirring constantly, for a few minutes, until slightly softened.

2. Add green beans, pepper, and salt, and cook a few minutes more, enough to take the raw edge off. Green beans should still be crispy.

3. Turn off heat, stir in coconut, and serve with rice.

Lime-Masala Mushrooms

(20 minutes, serves 4)

Another one of my own invention; quick and easy to make. Rich in butter, a favorite of hobbits and my dinner guests. This one is easy to start going and then just stir every once in a while as it cooks, so it's convenient for a dinner party when you have twelve things going at once!

1 ½ lbs. mushrooms, sliced or quartered
1 stick salted butter
½ rounded tsp. salt, or to taste
1 tsp. black pepper
1 tsp. Sri Lankan curry powder
¼ cup lime juice, or to taste

1. Sauté mushrooms in butter and salt and cook on high heat until quite reduced, stirring frequently.

2. Add curry powder, pepper, and lime juice and cook until juice is absorbed. Mushrooms should be glistening and slightly fried, not sitting in liquid. Serve hot with rice and curries. (Also nice on toast, or with breakfast eggs.)

Vegetable and Lentil Stew / Sambar

(45 minutes, serves 8)

This vegetable-lentil stew is a very malleable dish—make it with whichever vegetables please you, though pumpkin, okra, eggplant, drumsticks, and tomatoes are traditional. You can also vary the types of lentils used, and the spice level—some people leave the chili and pepper out entirely, some make it quite spicy. This version is somewhere in between, and makes for a healthy protein-packed breakfast or light dinner served with idli, thosai, or rice, and a little coconut chutney.

If you need it ready in a hurry, you can prepare sambar in a pressure cooker, just throwing everything in, but if you do it in stages as below, you'll get more richness of flavor.

Note: I don't recommend using potato if you plan to freeze some of it, as the potato will turn mealy on freezing. Otherwise, sambar generally freezes well.

> 2 small Japanese eggplants or one large globe eggplant, cubed
> 1 tsp. salt
> 1 tsp. ground turmeric
> ½ cup red lentils (masoor dal)
> 2 cups pumpkin (or winter squash)
> 2 carrots
> 1 drumstick, cut into 3-inch pieces

1 red onion, diced

1 Tbsp. ginger, minced

3 cloves garlic, chopped

4-6 cups water, as needed to cover vegetables

1 cup green beans, chopped

1 cup tomato, chopped

1 tsp. tamarind paste

1 tsp. salt

1 tsp. black pepper

2 Tbsp. sambar powder

1 ½ Tbsp. oil or ghee

6-8 okra, sliced

2 cups mushrooms, quartered

for tempering:

1 ½ Tbsp. oil or ghee

½ tsp. black mustard seed

½ tsp. split urad dal (black gram / matpe bean / ulunththu)

2 dried red chilies

1 stalk curry leaves

1. In a medium bowl, mix eggplant with salt and turmeric and set aside. (This draws the bitterness out of the eggplant.)

2. Put dal, pumpkin, carrots, drumstick, onion, ginger, garlic, and water in a large pot and bring to a boil; turn to medium-high and let cook about ten minutes, stirring periodically. If the water boils off too much, add more—you're aiming for a watery stew / thick soup in the end.

3. Add green beans, tomato, tamarind paste, salt, black pepper, and sambar powder; cook another ten minutes.

4. While sambar is cooking, in a separate frying pan, heat oil or ghee, then add okra and fry for a few minutes, stirring. Add mushrooms and continue to stir.

5. Drain any water from eggplant, blotting with a paper towel, and then add eggplant to pan and fry for a few minutes more. Add okra, mushrooms, and eggplant to the large pot of sambar, and continue to simmer, adding water if needed.

6. Tempering stage:
   heat remaining oil in the same frying pan on medium-low; add mustard seeds and urad dal and sauté, stirring, for a few minutes, until seeds begin to pop and dal turns a dark reddish-brown. Add dry chilies and curry leaves; sauté until the leaves become crisp and the chilies have darkened.

7. Stir in tempered seasonings to the pot of sambar, adding water if needed to desired thickness. Taste and add salt if needed. Serve hot, with idli, thosai, or rice.

Mambalam, nala mambalam,
Mama than tha mambalam,
Munjel vunai mambalam,
Munum vesum mambalam.

Mango, nice mango,
Uncle gave me a mango,
It is a yellow mango,
A sweet-smelling mango.

—Tamil children's rhyme

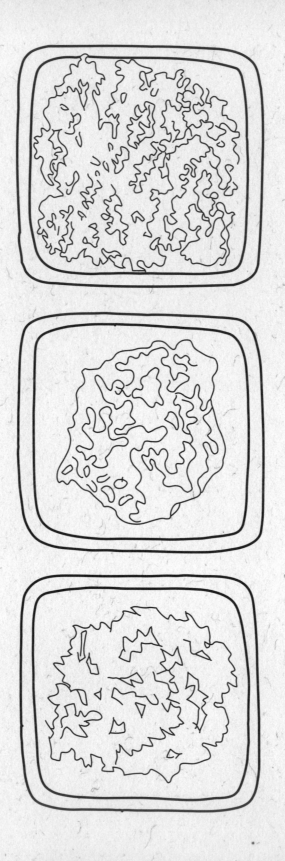

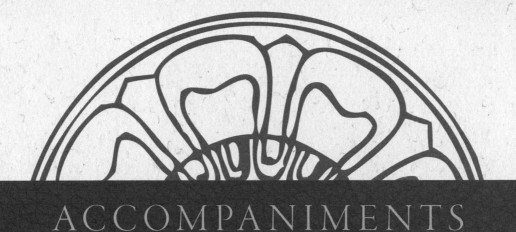

ACCOMPANIMENTS

Cucumber Salad

Pickled Beet Salad

Green Coconut Chutney / Thengai Chutney

Mango-Ginger Chutney

Bitter Gourd Sambol / Paavakkai Sambol

Chili Onion Sambol / Lunu Miris Sambol

Coconut Sambol / Thengai-Poo, or Pol Sambol

Eggplant Sambol / Kaththarikkai Sambol

Kale Sambol

Sweet Onion Sambol / Seeni Sambol

Coconut Milk Gravy / Sothi

Coriander Soup / Kothamalli Rasam

Cucumber-Tomato Raita

Leeks Fried with Chili

Mango Pickle / Maankai Oorukkai

ACCOMPANIMENTS

If you're short on time, rice, a vegetable, and possibly a meat is a sufficient Sri Lankan meal—but traditionally, you would also enjoy at least one or two accompaniments: sambols, chutneys, pickles, salads, and more. They tend to be intensely flavored, and bring balance and excitement to a plate, making it possible for everyone at the table to balance the meal to their own tastes, adding a little sweetness, chili heat, bitter tang, and more.

Sambols and salads can be cooked very quickly. Once you put the rice on, you still usually have time to make one or two of these while the rice is cooking. Others, such as chutneys and pickles, are best made in advance, and will keep for a long time in the fridge (or store unopened in the pantry, if properly sealed). They serve quite a few people—each person is meant to just take a little bit.

Of course, you can't guarantee that people will hold to that! Many of my friends tend to treat coconut sambol like a vegetable and just pile it on their plate. You can do that too, if you like, remembering that coconut is full of rich, fatty goodness.

Oh, and if you or your friends find spicy heat challenging, some cucumber-tomato raita is an essential palate-cooler. A glass of milk or mango lassi also helps. Remember— water only spreads the fire.

Cucumber Salad

(5 minutes, serves 8)

A cool, refreshing bite, slightly crisp.

> 1 English cucumber (or 2 Persian cucumbers), sliced into bite-size pieces
> ½ cup thinly sliced onion
> 1 green chili, chopped fine
> ¼ tsp. salt
> ¼ tsp. freshly ground black pepper
> ¼ tsp. sugar
> 1 Tbsp. lime juice or rice vinegar
> 2 Tbsp. coconut milk
> 1 tsp. ground Maldive fish (optional)

Combine and serve with rice or uppuma, and meat or vegetable curry, with perhaps a nice mango pickle on the side.

Pickled Beet Salad

(30 minutes, serves 8)

A sweet-sour accompaniment that can be eaten fresh; the flavors will mellow and blend if allowed to sit for a few days.

Note: Half a red onion, sliced and added at step 3, would grace this dish nicely.

> 2 cups raw beet, peeled, cut in half, and sliced
> 4 tsp. cumin seeds
> 1 tsp. salt
> ¼ cup sugar
> 1 cup vinegar

1. In a saucepan, boil beets in water; cook until beets are tender, about 10-15 minutes.

2. Sauté cumin seeds in a dry pan for a few minutes, stirring, until they start to smell fragrant. Remove from heat.

3. Drain beets, return to saucepan, combine with remaining ingredients and cumin seeds, bring to a boil, and simmer 10-15 minutes.

4. You can now cool and serve immediately with rice and curries, or alternatively, let cool, pour beets and liquid into a jar, close, and refrigerate. Eat within a few weeks (unless you follow proper procedures for long-term canning).

Green Coconut Chutney / Thengai Chutney

(10 minutes, serves 8)

This accompaniment adds a fresh, tangy element to a South Asian meal. If you'd like it to be more green (as some people prefer), you can add cilantro or parsley. This is typically served 'wet', along with idli / thosai and sambar. As it sits, the coconut will absorb more liquid; it is also tasty in its drier (though still moist) form.

> 1 cup fresh / frozen grated coconut (if using desiccated,
>   add 3 Tbsp. coconut milk)
> 1 onion, chopped
> 1 Tbsp. ginger, chopped
> 3 cloves garlic
> 1-3 green chilies
> about 10 curry leaves
> 1 tsp. salt
> 1 Tbsp. lime juice
> water as needed

Combine ingredients in food processor and pulse until well blended, about 5 minutes total. Add water as needed. Stop and scrape down sides as needed. Serve room temperature.

Mango-Ginger Chutney

(45 minutes, serves 8)

Y ou don't actually need to cook a chutney—you can just chop up some fruit and mix it with spices and serve; that would be common in Sri Lanka. But I prefer a more blended chutney, with a mellower flavor. A great quick appetizer for a party is serving this with crackers and cheddar cheese.

> 3 fresh mangoes, peeled and chopped (a ripe, 12 oz. mango will
>   produce about 1 cup of fruit)
> 1 rounded tsp. salt
> 1 cup malt vinegar
> 3 dried chilies (optional)
> 3 Tbsp. fresh ginger, peeled and chopped fine
> ¾ - 1 cup sugar
> ⅓ cup sultanas (golden raisins)
> 1 rounded tsp. Sri Lankan curry powder

1. Put mango pieces in a large bowl and sprinkle with salt.

2. Remove stalks and seeds from chilies (if used) and soak chilies in a little vinegar for 10 minutes. Combine vinegar, ginger, and chilies in a blender and blend (you can alternatively pound the chilies with a mortar and pestle and grate the ginger in).

3. Put blended mixture in a stainless steel pan with curry powder and sugar and bring to a boil. Simmer, uncovered, for 15 minutes.

4. Add mangoes and sultanas. Turn heat back to medium-high and cook, stirring occasionally, until thick and syrupy.

5. Cool and serve with rice and curries, or add to a sandwich—it's great with grilled chicken or pork. You can also use the slightly more liquid version as a salad dressing.

Note: You can substitute green apples, pears, apricots, etc. for mangoes. Or mix and match!

Note 2: If not eating immediately, store in a jar in the fridge for a few weeks, or in the pantry for months, if canned and sterilized properly.

Bitter Gourd Sambol / Paavakkai Sambol

(15 minutes + 1 hour draining time, serves 8)

Bitter gourd is quite bitter! Seasoning it with turmeric and salt will draw the bitterest water to the surface to be blotted off, and deep-frying also tempers the bitterness. But still, a hint remains, adding an unusual flavor to this accompaniment.

1 bitter gourd, sliced thin (about 2 cups)
1 tsp. ground turmeric
1 tsp. salt
1 dozen curry leaves
¼ red onion, sliced
6 cherry tomatoes, sliced
3 green chilies, chopped
oil for deep frying

1. Mix bitter gourd with turmeric and salt and let sit for an hour. Drain and blot dry with paper towels.

2. Heat oil and deep fry first the curry leaves, and then the bitter gourd in batches, removing to plates lined with paper towels.

3. Mix fried bitter gourd with tomatoes, chilies, and curry leaves and serve with rice and curries.

Chili Onion Sambol /
Lunu Miris Sambol

(10 minutes, serves 8)

This classic Sri Lankan sambol is a simple way to add heat and tang to any meal.

> 1 onion, chopped coarsely
> 3 dried red chilies
> 1-2 tsp. cayenne
> 1-2 tsp. lime juice
> 1 tsp. salt

Combine ingredients in a food processor (alternatively, mince onion fine and then combine ingredients with mortar and pestle). Serve with hoppers, thosai, or whatever you like. Great on sandwiches too!

Coconut Sambol / Thengai-Poo or Pol Sambol

(10 minutes, serves 8)

This is meant to be an accompaniment—make a batch (it keeps for weeks in the fridge) and then put a teaspoon or two on your plate with your rice / bread and curries. In Sri Lanka, they would just use straight up cayenne, instead of a mix of cayenne and paprika, which would make it fiercely spicy. If I were only going to make one accompaniment for the rest of my life, pol sambol would be my choice, although seeni sambol would be a very close second.

> 1 cup desiccated unsweetened coconut
> 3 Tbsp. hot milk (I heat mine in the microwave)
> 1 rounded tsp. salt
> 1 rounded tsp. cayenne
> 2 rounded tsp. paprika
> 2-3 Tbsp. lime juice, to taste
> 1 medium onion, minced fine

1. Reconstitute coconut in a large bowl with the hot milk. I recommend using your fingers to squeeze the milk through the coconut. (If you can get fresh or frozen grated coconut, that is, of course, even better, and you can skip this step.)

2. Add salt, cayenne, paprika, lime juice, and onion. Mix thoroughly with your hand, rubbing ingredients together until well blended.

Note: If you don't feel that your onion is minced sufficiently fine (ideally, to match the texture of the coconut), you can use a food processor to chop it more finely, or grind it with a mortar and pestle. You can grind just the onions, or the whole mixture.

Eggplant Sambol /
Kaththarikkai Sambol

(1 hour prep, 20 minutes cooking, serves 8)

My vegetarian friends are particularly fond of this dish. It offers a bright note, with its raw onion and lime juice, that wakes up a plate of rice and curry.

1 eggplant
1 rounded tsp. salt
1 rounded tsp. ground turmeric
oil for deep frying
3 fresh green chilies, sliced thin
1 medium onion, sliced thin
lime juice
¼ cup coconut milk, optional

1. Cut eggplant into quarters lengthwise and then slice thinly. Rub with salt and turmeric, spread on a few layers of paper towels and leave at least 1 hour. Bitter water will rise to the surface of the eggplant; blot that water with more paper towels. This will make for much tastier eggplant.

2. Heat about an inch of oil in a deep frying pan and fry eggplant slices slowly until brown on both sides. Lift out with Chinese spider (mesh metal spoon) and put in a dry bowl.

3. Mix with remaining ingredients; serve warm.

Kale Sambol

(20 minutes, serves 8)

I had never been a big kale fan, but my friend, Roshani, completely converted me with her Aunty Indranee's use of kale in this traditional sambol. In Sri Lanka, this would have been made with a native green, gotu kola, but kale is an excellent substitute (you can also try any other leafy greens, like beet greens, mustard greens, or rainbow chard).

For this preparation, kale is chopped small and tenderized with lime juice. When mixed with the coconut, tomatoes, sugar, and salt, the result is a tasty and addictive sambol that has become an essential component to many of our meals—if I make a meat curry now, I almost always make kale sambol to accompany it, and will often eat more sambol than curry. I'd have it with a little rice, but Kevin likes to just have beef curry and kale sambol together in a bowl, straight-up, which is also delicious.

Note: This can be served immediately, but best if allowed to sit and blend for an hour or so. It will keep in the fridge for a good week—refresh with a little extra lime juice as needed.

1 bunch kale, leaves stripped off (stems discarded)
1 medium onion, minced
1 cup shredded unsweetened coconut
1-2 cups cherry tomatoes, chopped

juice of 2 small limes (about 2-3 Tbsp.)
1-2 Tbsp. sugar
1 tsp. fine salt

1. Pulse kale in food processor until completely shredded into small bits.

2. Add onion, coconut, tomato, lime juice, sugar, salt. Mix thoroughly.

Sweet Onion Sambol / Seeni Sambol

(1 hour, serves 8)

The Sri Lankan version of caramelized onions is sweet, spicy, and tangy. It's important to cook the onions slowly—all the liquid in the onion must evaporate if you want the sambol to keep well. Made properly, this dish can keep for several weeks in the fridge, so you can enjoy a little with each curry meal for quite a long time. An essential accompaniment for hoppers, and delicious with many other meals.

½ cup vegetable oil
1 Tbsp. Maldive fish, powdered (optional)
4 medium onions, finely sliced
2 rounded tsp. cayenne
1 1-inch cinnamon stick
3 cloves
3 cardamom pods
1 stalk curry leaves
1 tsp. salt, or to taste
2 Tbsp. tamarind pulp
2 Tbsp. sugar

1. Heat oil in a large frying pan and start sautéing onions on medium-low (with Maldive fish, if using). Add cinnamon, cloves, cardamom, curry leaves, and chill powder; continue cooking, stirring occasionally, until soft and transparent, about 30 minutes.

2. After about 30 minutes, cover pan, and simmer 10 minutes.

3. Uncover pan and continue simmering, stirring occasionally, until liquid evaporates and oil starts to separate from other ingredients. Season to taste with salt.

4. Remove from heat, stir in sugar and tamarind pulp, and allow to cool before putting in a clean dry jar. Use in small quantities.

Coconut Milk Gravy / Sothi

(45 minutes + soaking time, serves 8)

This is a delicious traditional accompaniment for stringhoppers, served with a little coconut sambol. When I last visited Sri Lanka, that was one of my favorite meals to have for breakfast, in the very early morning at the hotel, while I was still jet-lagged. It's quite soothing. This makes a fairly large quantity, suitable for feeding several people; just cut ingredients in half for a smaller portion.

1-4 Tbsp. fenugreek seeds, soaked for two hours beforehand
1 Tbsp. toasted rice powder (optional)
1 large onion, diced
12 curry leaves
1 2-inch cinnamon stick
2 fresh green chilies, seeded and chopped
½ tsp. ground turmeric
1 tsp. salt
2 cups water
1 russet potato, peeled and cubed (optional)
3 cups coconut milk
4 hard-boiled eggs, cut in half lengthwise (optional)
1-2 Tbsp. lime juice, to taste

Note: Traditionally, this dish was made with quite a lot of fenugreek; modern recipes tend to reduce to about 1 tablespoon, instead of 4. But fenugreek is a potent galactagogue, so if you're making this dish for a nursing mother, you may want to go old-school.

Note 2: Toasted rice powder is used through Asia (especially in Thai cooking) to thicken and add flavor and fragrance to dishes. It's best made fresh, in the quantities needed. To make, take 1 tablespoon rice and sauté over medium heat in a dry pan for 10-15 minutes, stirring constantly. It'll release a beautifully nutty, toasted scent. Then grind to a powder—I use a coffee grinder that I keep dedicated for spices, but you could also use a food processor, or the traditional mortar and pestle.

1. Put all the ingredients except the last three (coconut milk, eggs, and lime juice) in a saucepan. Bring to a boil, then turn down heat and simmer, covered, until onions are reduced to a pulp and the potatoes are cooked, about 30 minutes.

2. Stir well, add thick coconut milk and heat without bringing dish to a boil. Stir in lime juice, and/or additional salt to taste, and then carefully add the eggs. Simmer a minute or two longer, stirring, and then serve hot, with stringhoppers or rice.

Coriander Soup / Kothamalli Rasam

(20 minutes, serves 8)

I don't make this often myself, but it's one of my mother's favorite dishes. For a very simple meal, serve it to sip with plain rice, with perhaps a little sambol. It's lovely when you're feeling a little under the weather; the tang and slight spiciness are just the thing to settle you.

1 Tbsp. tamarind paste
1 cup hot water
2 cloves garlic, sliced
¾ rounded tsp. freshly ground black pepper
1 rounded tsp. ground cumin
4 cups cold water
2 rounded tsp. salt
2 Tbsp. chopped fresh coriander / cilantro leaf
2 tsp. vegetable oil
2 Tbsp. coriander seeds
1 rounded tsp. black mustard seed
8 curry leaves

1. Dissolve tamarind paste in hot water.

2. Put tamarind liquid, garlic, pepper, cumin, water, salt, and coriander leaves into a saucepan and bring it to a boil.

3. Turn heat down and simmer for 10 minutes.

4. In another pan, heat the oil and sauté the coriander seeds, mustard seeds, and curry leaves until leaves are toasted. Add to the simmering liquid and serve hot.

Cucumber-Tomato Raita

(10 minutes, serves 8)

I'm afraid I've never picked up the habit myself of eating yogurt with curry, but many of my friends swear by raita, and the ones who have trouble with the spiciness of some of the dishes really appreciate the cooling properties of yogurt. I often make some raita to accompany a spicy meal when serving guests.

> 1 medium cucumber
> 2-4 plum tomatoes, chopped coarsely
> 2 fresh green chilies, seeded
>   and chopped (optional)
> ½ tsp. salt
> freshly ground black pepper to taste
> 1 cup yogurt (ideally full-fat)

1. Grate cucumber coarsely; squeeze out excess water.

2. Mix all ingredients well; serve cold.

185

Leeks Fried with Chili

(50 minutes, serves 8)

This accompaniment offers a little extra heat and onion-y zing to a plate of rice and curry.

> 4 medium leeks
> ¼ cup oil
> ½ rounded tsp. ground turmeric
> 1 ½ rounded tsp. cayenne
> 1 rounded tsp. salt

1. Rinse dirt off outside of leeks. Discard any tough or withered leaves, but do use the green portions as well as the white.

2. With a sharp knife, slice the leeks thinly across the stalk, making thin rings / chiffonade; when you're slicing the green leaves, make a tight bundle in your hands for easier slicing.

3. Wash the sliced leeks very thoroughly. The soil trapped between the leaves won't actually taste particularly bad, but the grittiness is unpleasant. I recommend not simply running the sliced leeks under a colander—rather, put them in a large bowl of water and wash them vigorously, changing the water at least three times. This is labor-intensive, but well worth it.

4. Heat oil in a large saucepan and add the leeks. Sauté, stirring for 5 minutes, then add the remaining ingredients and stir until well blended.

5. Cover and cook over low heat for 30 minutes, stirring occasionally. The leeks will reduce in volume. Uncover and cook, stirring, until liquid evaporates and leeks appear slightly oily. Serve hot.

Mango Pickle /
Maankai Oorukkai

(20 minutes, serves 8)

This is a fiery, fruity accompaniment that will keep refrigerated for a long time—you can add a little to your plate of rice and curry whenever you want to kick things up a bit. It's also tasty with cheese and crackers, or layered in a sandwich with roast meat, and it makes a terrific addition to a grilled cheese sandwich.

2 cups raw mango (about 2 large), cubed small
3 Tbsp. oil or ghee
6-8 curry leaves
1 Tbsp. black mustard seed
1 Tbsp. ginger, chopped fine
1 Tbsp. garlic, chopped fine
3 green chilies, chopped
3 Tbsp. cayenne
1 tsp. ground turmeric
¼ cup vinegar
1 cup water
1 tsp. salt

1. Heat oil in a large frying pan and sauté mustard seeds, curry leaves, ginger, garlic, and chili in oil or ghee on medium-high for a few minutes, stirring, until they start to smell cooked instead of raw.

2. Add cayenne, turmeric, vinegar, water, and salt; cook down to a thick pickling paste, about five minutes. Turn off heat and allow to cool for fifteen minutes or so.

3. Add mango to pan and mix well to combine. Store in the fridge and eat within a year or so, or fill canning jars and seal properly for seriously long-term storage). Serve with congee or other mild dishes.

Come to me.
I will make you rice.

Thick, white, sticky rice,
clinging to your fingertips.
Dark, wild rice,
scented like fields in autumn.

Slender grains of basmati rice,
aromatic, rich with rose essence,
saffron-gold-threaded,
graced by sultanas,
by almonds and cashews...

Come to me, and I will feed you rice
made by my own small hands.

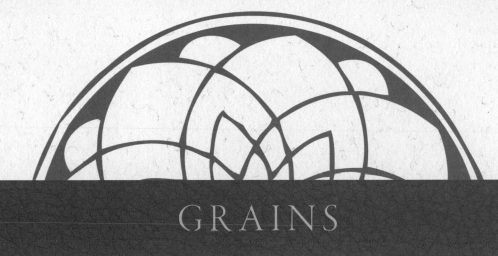

GRAINS

Bombay Toast / Bombatoast

Chopped Roti Stir-Fry / Kottu Roti

Golden Rice Pilaf

Herbal Porridge / Kola Kenda

Hoppers / Appam

Lamb Biryani (or Goat, Beef, or Chicken)

Noodles

Plain Roti / Kothambu Roti

Red Rice Congee

Savory Rice Pancakes / Thosai

Steamed Rice Cakes / Idli

Steamed Rice Flour and Coconut / Pittu

Steamed Rice Flour and Coconut with Milk / Pal Pittu

Stir-Fried Semolina / Uppuma

Stringhoppers / Idiyappam

Stringhopper Biryani / Idiyappam Biryani

Bombay Toast / Bombatoast

(15-20 minutes, serves 4)

Buttery-sweet bombatoast is one of my favorite breakfast foods. The term comes from Bombay toast, like French toast, but the Sri Lankan version has sugar in the mix, so you don't need syrup. There are savory versions too, with onion and green chili, but this is the one I grew up eating. It's soft and tears apart as you eat it; my children love it too.

It's the perfect meal for recuperating from an illness.

> 12 slices white bread (not too mushy, or it'll completely fall apart)
> 2 cups milk
> 2 eggs
> 6 Tbsp. sugar (this makes it pretty sweet; you could cut back a bit
>   if you wanted)
> butter for spreading

1. Butter both sides of each slice of bread. (You can do these as you go, pretty much.)

2. Beat the egg well and add sugar; beat well until sugar dissolves. Add mix to milk and beat well.

3. Dip a slice of bread in the egg and milk batter (both sides) and put it in hot buttered griddle (I'd use nonstick). (If you leave in the batter too long, it'll get soggy and hard to flip without tearing. Still yummy, though.)

4. After a bit (when you think it's browned, but not burned), flip and cook the other side. Serve hot.

Chopped Roti Stir-Fry / Kottu Roti

(30 minutes, serves 4)

This is one of my favorite Sri Lankan dishes, though I don't make it with as much flair as the street vendors, who wield massive knives chopping at furious speed. The curry sauce blends perfectly with the roti and the fresh vegetables, creating a soft, tender concoction.

4 rotis (or parathas or similar flatbreads), chopped coarsely
2-3 Tbsp. vegetable oil
1 red onion, chopped
3 green chilies, chopped
1 stalk curry leaves
2 eggs, beaten with 1 tsp. salt and ½ tsp. pepper
1 cup green beans, chopped small
1 carrot, grated coarsely
1 leek, sliced thinly (green and white parts), rinsed thoroughly
1 cup leftover curry (meat or vegetarian, but it needs to have at
  least ½ cup of sauce)

1. Sauté onion, green chilies, and curry leaves in oil until lightly browned, about five minutes.

2. Add eggs and fry, stirring to break up the eggs.

3. Add green beans, carrot, and leeks, and sauté until cooked through, about five more minutes.

4. Add rotis and mix thoroughly.

5. Add curry and mix thoroughly. Serve hot!

Note: As a variation, you can add half a chopped cabbage at step three, and reduce the amount of roti, for a more vegetal approach.

Note 2: I've made this with tortillas in a pinch, but rotis do a better job of sopping up the sauce. Naan is a little thick, so is not ideal, but if you're desperate and have nothing else on hand, needs must.

197

Golden Rice Pilaf

(20 minutes, serves 4-6)

Here's where I cheat. When I'm having a party, I'd often like to serve biryani, as my mother would—but making biryani properly is a fair bit of work, and sometimes I just don't have time. So I often make this instead.

> 2 cups uncooked basmati rice
> 4 cups water
> ¼ - ½ cup sultanas (golden raisins)
> ¼ - ½ cup cashews
> 1 Tbsp. butter
> ¼ tsp. salt
> 1-2 drops rose essence
> ½ tsp. saffron (you can use turmeric for a similar color,
>   but it won't taste right)

1. Combine all ingredients in a large pot and bring to a boil.

Note: This is truly low-effort cooking—a tastier approach would be to sauté the cashews and sultanas in the butter (with maybe a little sliced onion) in a separate pan, and then stir those into the cooked rice at the end, saving some to garnish the top of the dish with some fresh chopped coriander leaves.

2. Cover and turn heat down to simmer until rice is cooked, approximately 15 minutes.

Herbal Porridge /
Kola Kenda

(5-10 minutes, plus time to cook rice, serves 4)

This herbal leaf porridge is considered tremendously healthful, and is often drunk straight up first thing in the morning in Sri Lanka, or mixed with rice for a light breakfast. It's typically lightly seasoned—the fresh herbs carry the flavor, with just a little salt and a touch of black pepper. But you can amend it as desired—fresh ginger is a common addition, and if you prefer a sweeter breakfast, you can always stir in a little jaggery.

Kola kenda is supposed to stave off all manner of digestive difficulties, but I'm enough of a gardener to find those claims unlikely, given that the choice of herbs is so variable. But a quick internet search will find far more detail on the subject, if you're so inclined. It's a staple of the Ayurvedic medicine tradition. Regardless of the health claims, it's a fresh and tasty start to your day.

You can buy powdered versions of the traditional herbs found in Sri Lanka online, the result looks rather unappealing and murky, compared to the brightness of fresh herbs. I use a combination of fresh curry leaves, cilantro, and fenugreek (from a frozen packet), but you can experiment with the dark leafy herbs of your choice. Straight-up cilantro works fine, for example.

Traditional herbs would include gotu kola (Centella asiatica), sessile joyweed (Alternanthera sessilis), known as mukunuwenna in Sri Lanka, haathawariya (Asparagus racemosus), welpenela [Cardiospermum Halicacabum (Sapindaceae)], aubergine (Elabatu), or polpala (Aerva lanata).

1 bunch fresh herbs (about 1 ½ cups)
1 cup coconut milk
2 cups water
1 tsp. salt
½ tsp. pepper (optional)
1 cup cooked rice (I use red samba rice)
2-3 Tbsp. jaggery (optional)

1. Combine herbs with coconut milk and water in blender and puree until smooth. (Traditionally, the herbs would have been mashed with a mortar and pestle.) Add salt, and pepper if using.

2. Stir herbal soup into rice in a pot, bring to a boil, then turn it down and simmer for a few minutes, stirring, until well blended. Serve hot, with jaggery if desired.

Hoppers / Appam

(30-45 minutes + overnight fermenting time, makes 12)

If I had to pick the perfect Sri Lankan meal, this would be it. There's nothing like breaking off a crisp piece of hopper, dipping it into broken egg, and scooping up some curry and a bit of seeni sambol. Delectable.

These rice flour pancakes have a unique shape; fermented batter is swirled in a special small hemispherical pan, so you end up with a soft, spongy center, and lacey, crispy sides—that contrast is the true glory of the hopper. Typically you'd make one egg hopper per person, plus another plain hopper or two, and maybe a sweet hopper to finish up.

Note: You can buy instant hopper mix, available online, and just add water, which will work fine, and doesn't require overnight planning ahead. Many diasporic Sri Lankans I know use that option regularly.

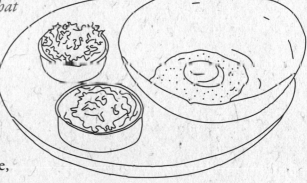

If you don't have a hopper pan, you can make hoppers in a regular frying pan; you just won't get quite as much of the crispy sides. It's a little time-consuming to make hoppers, since each one must be individually steamed for a few minutes, but with practice, you can have four hopper pans going on a stove at once. I'd recommend starting with just one pan at a time, though! Serve with curry and seeni sambol.

> 2 cups South Asian rice flour (or a mix of rice and wheat flour)
> 1 tsp. sugar
> pinch of baking powder
> ½ tsp. salt
> 2 cups coconut milk
> eggs for egg hoppers
> extra coconut milk and jaggery for sweet hoppers

1. Mix first five ingredients thoroughly in a large bowl, cover, and set in a warm, turned-off oven to ferment overnight. (In a cold climate, fermentation may not occur without a little help—I turn my oven on to 250°, and when it's reached temperature, turn it off and put the covered bowl in the oven to stay warm.)

2. Mix again, adding water if necessary to make a quite thin, pourable batter.

3. Heat pan (grease if not non-stick) on medium, and when it's hot, pour about ⅓ cup batter into the center. Pick up the pan immediately and swirl the batter around, coating the cooking surface. The sides of the hopper should end up with holes in them: thin, lacy, and crisp—if the batter is coating the pan more thickly, mix in some hot water to thin it down. Cover and let cook for 2-4 minutes— you'll know it's ready when the sides have started to brown and the center is thoroughly cooked. A silicone spatula will help get the hopper out of the pan.

4. For egg hoppers, after swirling, crack an egg in the center before covering. The egg will cook as the hopper does, finishing in about 3-4 minutes.

5. For sweet hoppers, after swirling, add a tablespoon of coconut milk and a teaspoon of jaggery to the center of the pan, then cook as usual.

Lamb Biryani

(or Goat, Beef, Chicken, Prawns, Vegetables...)

(1 hour, serves 6-8)

Biryani is a rice-based dish made with spices and either lamb, goat, beef, chicken, egg, prawns, or vegetables—your choice! The word *biryani* comes from Hindi and Persian words meaning "roasted." Biryani is generally more strongly spiced than a pilaf (though closely related), and commonly layered as part of its preparation. Sri Lankan biryani is spicier than Indian, and generally served with curries and sambols.

This has a lot of ingredients and may look a bit intimidating, but it's actually quite straightforward—mostly, you're just adding everything to one big pot, step-by-step. It isn't usually everyday food, given that it does take a while to cook, but if you have a special occasion to celebrate, biryani is an impressive crowd-pleaser. It will come out a bit dry, so I would serve it with a curry, or something else that offers a gravy. Even a yogurt raita would work!

Note: If you don't have an oven-safe dutch oven, you can start this in a regular large pot and transfer it to a baking dish for the final step.

2 cups basmati rice
2 lbs. lamb (or other meat / poultry / fish) – omit for vegetarian version
1 tsp. ground coriander
1 tsp. ground cumin

1 tsp. black pepper
1 tsp. Sri Lankan curry powder
1 tsp. salt
1 Tbsp. vinegar
4 Tbsp. butter or ghee
1 cup cashews
1 cup sultanas (golden raisins)
3 sliced onions
8-12 curry leaves
6 cardamom pods
6 cloves
1 2-inch cinnamon stick, broken in 3-6 pieces
1 cup thick coconut milk
4 boiled eggs, peeled and sliced in half

1. Cook rice via usual method and set aside.

2. Cut lamb into cubes and season with coriander, cumin, black pepper, curry powder, salt, and vinegar and set aside.

3. Melt butter or ghee over medium heat and lightly fry the cashews and sultanas, stirring, and set aside.

4. In the same pan, fry the onions, curry leaves, cardamom pods, and cloves until golden brown.

5. Add the lamb to the pan and sauté, stirring occasionally, until the lamb is cooked through and the liquid has cooked off, about 20 minutes.

6. Add the rice and stir gently; add coconut milk and cinnamon, mixing gently. Simmer over a low flame for about five minutes, until well blended.

7. Serve on a flat dish and decorate with fried sultanas, cashews, and boiled egg halves.

Note: For a fancy preparation, I've read that some chefs fry papadum, cut it fine, until it resembles straw, and then use that to concoct a nest; they nestle the biryani with it, and mold chickens out of a combination of mashed potato, butter, and egg yolk. But I've never seen or tried that!

Vegetarian variation: For richer flavor, cook rice in vegetable broth for step 1. Then skip steps 2 and 5, or for 5, sauté in your favorite chopped vegetables instead.

Noodles

(2 hours, serves dozens)

This is a classic festive holiday dish, which is in appearance similar to chow mein, and I suspect that, like our Chinese rolls, this dish was adapted from food made by Chinese laborers during colonial times. It can be made vegetarian easily, though my family is more likely to go in the other direction and incorporate at least 2-3 kinds of meat / shrimp.

It's a fair bit of labor, since we prep all the ingredients in separate batches for maximal flavor, but can mostly be done in advance (even months in advance), and just have 15 minutes of prep right before the party. These noodles also freeze well after being fully prepared, so we tend to make big batches, and freeze any extra for a rainy day.

oil for deep-frying
3 medium onions, onions, chopped fine, plus ¼ tsp. salt
1 lb. shredded carrots, plus ¼ tsp. salt
1 leek, sliced thinly (green and white parts), rinsed thoroughly,
  plus ½ tsp. salt and 3 Tbsp. oil
1 lb. dry beef curry
1 lb. dry shrimp curry
6 eggs, 2 Tbsp. butter
4 cups chicken broth, 4 cups water
1 cup sultanas (optional)

2 lbs. dry rice vermicelli noodles
2 Tbsp. butter
1 cup chopped roasted, salted cashews (optional)

1. Prep meat and shrimp curries in advance, if using. Set aside.

2. Deep-fry onions and salt in oil until crispy. (You can also sauté if preferred; it just won't be quite as crispy.) Remove with a slotted spoon to drain on a plate lined with paper towels. Set aside.

3. Repeat step 2 with shredded carrots and salt. Set aside.

4. Sauté leeks and salt in 3 tablespoons oil for 10-15 minutes, until softened. Set aside. *Note: All the previous ingredients can be prepped in advance and either refrigerated or even frozen.*

5. Scramble eggs in butter. Set aside.

6. Bring chicken broth, water, and sultanas to a rolling boil; add noodles and butter. Cook 3-5 minutes, until soft, stirring as needed. Drain.

7. Mix noodles with dry meat and/or shrimp, onions, carrots, leeks, eggs, and cashews, using either a wooden spoon or your clean hand. Serve hot, with a curry to accompany (something with a nice liquid gravy is best).

Plain Roti / Kothambu Roti

(30 minutes, serves 4-6)

> 1 cup all-purpose flour
> 1 ½ tsp. baking powder
> ¼ tsp. fine salt
> water (as required, around ½ cup)
> 1 cup vegetable oil (enough to submerge rotis)

1. Combine flour, baking powder, and salt in a bowl.

2. Add water slowly, then knead to make smooth dough, about 10 minutes (the dough should not be sticky). Divide into twelve portions and form little balls with the dough.

3. Pour oil into a flat tray; submerge balls in oil. (It's a lot of oil, but if you make roti regularly, you can save it and re-use it time after time.)

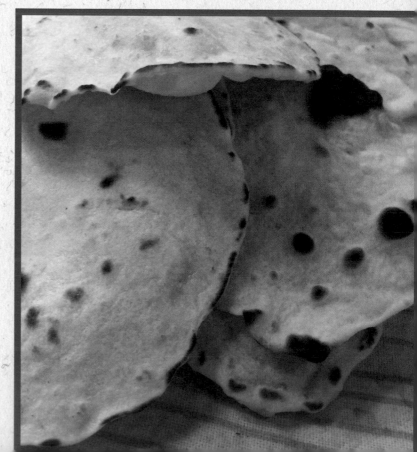

4. Heat a frying pan (either nonstick, or plan to drizzle a little oil in the pan as needed to prevent sticking). Take a ball of dough, flatten into a circle, and roll out until paper-thin—as thin as you can get it without tearing.

5. Cook each roti separately on high, turning over after about thirty seconds to cook the other side. They will brown slightly. Remove to a dishtowel, covering them each time, to keep warm. Serve either warm or at room temperature.

Red Rice Congee

(30 minutes, serves 2)

While many may associate 'congee' with a Chinese breakfast dish, the word 'congee' actually comes from the Tamil word 'kanji'; it refers to a rice-based porridge, eaten throughout Asia. This variation is a comforting way to start your morning—a traditional breakfast made either with fresh rice or leftover, and served with a little jaggery to sweeten it. It's also good for building up the strength of recovering invalids. Red rice can be purchased online, and is similar to brown rice in nutritional content. It has a mildly nutty flavor; a healthy choice for breakfast! You can make this with white or brown rice too, of course.

Some people prefer a more soupy version; just add more water at the end. Traditionally, you would smash the rice down with a spoon as a final step, to give it more of a porridge consistency, but personally, I prefer the distinct grains. Another option is to grind about half the cooked rice in a food processor after step 1, but that does mean one more thing to wash!

Other traditional accompaniments include fruit, nuts, or fiery luna miris sambol. This is a dish that easily adapts to your personal taste.

1 cup red rice
1 ¾ cups water
pinch of salt
2 Tbsp. ghee or vegetable oil
1 large onion, sliced thin

1 Tbsp. ginger, sliced thin
3 cloves garlic, sliced thin
2 green chilies, chopped
1 stalk curry leaves
1 tsp. salt
1 cup coconut milk
1 cup water
2-3 Tbsp. jaggery

1. In a pot, combine rice, 1 ¾ cups water, and pinch of salt. Bring to a boil, cover, cook 20 minutes, then turn off the heat and let sit 5 more minutes.

2. In a large frying pan, sauté onion, ginger, garlic, chilies, curry leaves, and salt in ghee, until onions are golden-brown.

3. Add rice to pan and mix well; add coconut milk and water and simmer a few minutes to desired thickness. Serve hot, with jaggery.

Savory Rice Pancakes / Thosai

(20 minutes + soaking, grinding, and fermenting time, serves 4)

Known as dosa in India, these tangy rice and lentil pancakes are delicious for breakfast or a light dinner, served with sambar and coconut chutney. For a more substantial version (masala thosai), add a spiced potato-onion filling.

You can make thosai from a just-add-water-and-oil mix, but making it from scratch is supposedly healthier, since it involves fermenting with wild bacteria.

½ cup idli or parboiled rice, washed
½ cup basmati rice, washed
1 cup split urad dal, washed
1 tsp. fenugreek seeds
1 tsp. salt

1. Mix rice, cover with water in a bowl. In a separate bowl, combine urad dal and fenugreek seeds, cover with water. Let soak for at least 4 hours.

2. Drain rice and grind in a food processor until very fine and smooth; add water if necessary. You're aiming for a thin pourable batter. Repeat with urad dal and fenugreek seeds.

3. Mix batters together in a large bowl with salt, cover, and set aside in a warm oven (turned off) overnight (or for at least 8 hours).

Note: If making masala thosai, make masala potatoes before cooking thosai; see below.

4. To make thosai, stir well, adding water if necessary to make a pourable batter.

5. Grease and heat a large frying pan on high; spoon about a half cup of batter (a ladle works well for this) onto the pan; spread it out with the back of the ladle to make a large circle.

6. Don't flip! When the bottom turns golden and crisp, and the top has thoroughly bubbled, use a spatula to remove from pan.

7. If making masala thosai, add a few spoons of potato mixture (below) to the center of the thosai; fold and serve hot, with chutney and sambar, or a vegetable curry.

Masala Potato Filling

> 1 lb. russet potatoes, boiled, peeled, and cubed
> 3 Tbsp. ghee or vegetable oil
> ½ tsp. split urad dal
> 1 tsp. black mustard seed
> 2 dozen curry leaves
> 1 large onion, chopped
> 5 green chilies, finely sliced
> 1 Tbsp. ginger, minced fine
> 3 cloves garlic, chopped
> 1 tsp. salt
> ½ tsp. ground turmeric

1. Heat oil in a large frying pan over medium; add urad dal, then mustard seeds, then curry leaves. Stir and fry for about thirty seconds.

2. Add the onion, green chilies, ginger, and garlic, and fry until golden-translucent.

3. Add salt and turmeric, stir for a few minutes more. Add the boiled potatoes and stir to combine, until they are well incorporated.

Steamed Rice Cakes / Idli

(40 minutes + soaking and fermenting time, makes 36)

Soft, warm, slightly tangy idli fresh from the steamer are a healthy breakfast option (one-third lentil to two-thirds rice). Typically you'd use a specialty device, an idli steamer, but there are video tutorials online showing how to improvise an idli steamer with tin foil (with holes poked in it). You can also steam it as a flat cake and cut squares of it to serve, or steam it in buttered four ounce ramekins.

I admit, I mostly make idli from a just-add-water-and-oil mix, which uses baking soda as a rising agent and takes about twenty minutes. But if you want to go old-school and use actual fermentation (which supposedly has more health benefits), you can easily make it from scratch. You'll need to start about a day in advance of when you plan to serve. A great choice for a casual brunch, served with sambar and coconut chutney.

> 1 cup split urad dal
> 2 cups idli or parboiled rice
> 1 tsp salt
> vegetable oil

1. In two bowls, soak dal and rice separately for eight hours. They will swell and expand notably, so leave room.

2. Drain rice and dal and grind both separately to a fine consistency. (A food processor will work fine.) Add water as needed; the ground rice will remain grainy, but should become a thick and pourable batter. The ground dal will turn into a dough on grinding.

3. Mix them together in a large bowl, using your clean hand to blend thoroughly. Add salt and mix in well.

4. Cover with a cloth and leave for eight hours or overnight to ferment. (In a cold climate, fermentation may not occur without a little help—I turn my oven on to 250°, and when it's reached temperature, turn it off and put the covered bowl in the oven to stay warm.)

5. Put some oil on a paper towel and grease the idli molds. Pour a spoonful of batter into each mold, filling them to the edge. Steam until they are cooked through, about 15-20 minutes; the idlis shouldn't be sticky to the touch; you're aiming for soft, but firm.

6. Remove from the mold and serve hot with coconut chutney and sambar.

Note: If you're having trouble with fermentation, adding a teaspoon of fenugreek or even a little yeast to the batter will help.

Steamed Rice Flour and Coconut / Arisi-Maa Pittu

(20 minutes, serves 4-6)

Pittu is one of many dishes we eat instead of rice, at breakfast, lunch, or dinner; it's tastiest when made with fresh coconut, but works just fine with reconstituted desiccated coconut. With sambol and a little curry, it's a perfect breakfast. We would make this in a bamboo or metal cylinder steamer; you can improvise a cylindrical steamer by using a tall narrow can (about the size of a coffee can) and punching holes in the bottom. But pittu also works fine in any regular steamer; it just won't have the characteristic cylindrical shape when served. Traditionally, pittu was made solely with rice flour, but combining with wheat flour gives a softer texture.

> 1 cup wheat flour
> 1 cup white or red rice flour
> 1 tsp salt
> boiling water as needed (about half a cup)
> 1 cup desiccated unsweetened coconut
> ¼ cup coconut milk

1. Combine flours and salt in a bowl and microwave for one minute. Check for clumping. If necessary, microwave another minute or two, until it starts to clump. This process makes it easier to mix the flour with water in the next step without forming lumps. (Alternatively, steam for a few minutes between two

layers of cheesecloth, or roast the flour in a pan, or use pre-steamed or pre-roasted flour.)

2. Add boiling water to bowl, a little at a time, and stir with a wooden spoon—you're aiming for a texture similar to crumble or rough cornmeal, sometimes called pittu pebbles.

3. In a separate bowl, combine the desiccated coconut and coconut milk; work gently with your fingers until all the coconut is well-moistened (if you're using fresh or frozen grated coconut, you can skip this step, as it's ready to use).

4. Fill steamer with mixture, alternating thick layers of pittu pebbles and thin layers of coconut (or you can simply mix the coconut and pittu pebbles together before filling steamer); press it down lightly.

5. Steam in a large pot over boiling water for 10-15 minutes, until dough is thoroughly cooked.
Push out onto a plate with a long wooden spoon and serve hot with curry and/or sambol and/or jaggery and coconut milk.

Steamed Rice Flour and Coconut with Milk / Pal Pittu

(20 minutes, serves 4-6)

P al pittu follows a similar recipe to pittu, but the steamed flour is mixed with sweetened coconut milk for a soft, soothing breakfast. A gentle start to your day. This is also a nice way to use up leftover pittu.

1 cup wheat flour
1 cup white or red rice flour
1 tsp. salt
boiling water as needed (about half a cup)
1 cup coconut milk
2 Tbsp. sugar

1. Combine flours and salt in a bowl and microwave for one minute. Check if clumping. If necessary, microwave another minute or two, until it starts to clump. This process makes it easier to mix the flour with water in the next step without forming lumps. (Alternatively, steam for a few minutes between two layers of cheesecloth, or roast the flour in a pan, or use pre-steamed or pre-roasted flour.)

2. Add boiling water to bowl, a little at a time, and stir with a wooden spoon—you're aiming for a texture similar to crumble or rough cornmeal, sometimes called pittu pebbles.

3. Fill steamer with pittu pebbles; press down lightly. Steam in a large pot over boiling water for 10-15 minutes, until dough is thoroughly cooked. Push out with a long wooden spoon and set aside.

4. In a small pot, bring remaining cup of coconut milk and sugar to a boil, then turn off heat. Add pittu and stir until milk is absorbed. Serve hot.

Stir-Fried Semolina / Uppuma

(20 minutes, serves 4-6)

When I was harried in grad school, I made a very fast, very simple version of this often—five minutes to boil water, add semolina with some butter and salt, stir, and serve. Served with spicy egg and mackerel curry, it's a wonderful breakfast or dinner; the soft uppuma blends beautifully with the fish—my ultimate comfort food.

This version, which is a little more time-consuming, offers more vegetables, more interesting seasonings, and a fluffier texture—it's tasty on its own, or with a vegetable or meat curry. Both versions are great!

2 Tbsp. butter
1 onion, chopped fine
3 dried red chili pods
1 tsp. black mustard seed
1 tsp. cumin seed
1 stalk curry leaves
1 rounded tsp. salt
2 carrots chopped small
½ cup peas (or chopped green beans)
3 cups water
2 cups coarse semolina

1. Roast semolina in a dry pan over medium-high heat, stirring constantly for about five minutes, until it's darkened slightly. This will give the end result a fluffier texture, with less clumping. Remove to a plate and set aside.

2. Sauté onions with seasonings in butter on medium-high for a few minutes.

3. Add carrots and continue to cook until carrots are softened and onions are golden-translucent. Add peas and cook a few minutes longer.

4. Add water; bring to a boil.

5. Turn down to a simmer and quickly pour in the semolina, stirring constantly, making sure all the wheat is moistened. Remove from heat and allow dish to sit for a few minutes before serving. Serve warm.

Note: You can use farina (sold as Cream of Wheat) instead of semolina for an almost identical result. Semolina comes from durum wheat (high in protein, produces more gluten). Farina comes from any hard wheat but durum.

Stringhoppers / Idiyappam

(20-30 minutes, serves 4)

This is a classic Sri Lankan breakfast food: beautifully soft steamed rice flour noodles, deliciously comforting when served with a mild sothi and a bright pol sambol. Idiyappam also make a nice light dinner, often accompanied by a little chicken curry or fish curry; other appropriate accompaniments include luna miris or seeni sambol, ambulthiyal, or jaggery. Idiyappam take some effort to prepare, but when done right, there is nothing to match them, and cooks take pride in making the softest, fluffiest strings.

In Sri Lanka, idiyappam are made with both rice flour and red rice flour. The heartier red rice flour has a little more flavor, but the white rice flour is gorgeously delicate; I can't pick a favorite. You can also buy 'idiyappam flour' already toasted and ready to go. If you have rice but no rice flour on hand, you can grind the rice yourself—in the old days, that would be done with a large mortar and pestle, but now an electric mill or coffee grinder will do the job, though you may need to run the flour through a fine sieve and re-grind portions until it is all of flour consistency. A thicker grain won't work for this preparation, as the dough won't be able to make its way through the tiny holes in the press. Wash the rice first, and spread it out on a clean dish towel to dry before grinding; generally thirty minutes should be sufficient.

Making idiyappam requires some specialized tools—you'll need a press, for one, with tiny holes to press the dough through. There are two basic kinds—one that you press down with both hands, and another that you crank; I find the latter notably easier, requiring less grip strength, though it does take a little practice to get the coordination down. They're both easily available online now, for around twenty dollars. (I tried using a potato ricer, but it didn't work well at all, and I don't think an Italian pasta maker would suffice either, though you could certainly try.) You also need a method for steaming the finished idiyappam—typically, you would use stringhopper mats designed for the purpose, though you can also steam them in an idli maker if you have one on hand, or on bamboo leaves.

When serving, it is best to eat this dish with your clean hand, so you can mix bites of idiyappam, sothi, and sambol together into little, perfect mouthfuls; eating with a fork will simply not give the tastiest results.

> 2 cups rice flour, white or red
> 1 tsp. salt
> 2 ½ cups boiling water, or as needed

1. Optional: Roast the flour in a dry pan over medium heat, stirring constantly, for five to eight minutes. This should improve the flavor slightly, and make the dough easier to work with; it's particularly useful in a humid climate, to prevent the flour from clumping as you work. It should be free-flowing, like salt, and the flour should not change color.

2. In the same pan or a large mixing bowl, stir in salt, and then add boiling water, a little at a time, mixing with a large wooden spoon. (Alternatively, this can be done in a stand mixer with the dough attachment; start slow so as not to spatter boiling water.) Continue adding water until it is starting to form a dough, then turn out onto a board and, as soon as it's cool enough to be worked, knead into a smooth dough. This is the trickiest part, and you may want to consult additional photos or videos online to get a sense of the correct consistency; it's hard to give exact measurements, since it's dependent on local humidity and other factors. The dough should be soft and not sticky; if it's hard, add a little more boiling water to soften it, and if it's sticky, add a little more rice flour (untoasted is fine).

3. Place the dough (you'll need to work in portions) in an idiyappam press and squeeze it onto idiyappam mats, using a circular motion to create the characteristic round nest of strings.

4. Place the idiyappam mats in a large steamer and steam 10-15 minutes, until the idiyappam are fully cooked; they should be springy in texture, but still soft. Remove from steamer and serve immediately with sothi and pol sambol.

Note: According to The Story of Our Food, *by Indian food historian K. T. Achaya, idiyappam has been around since at least the 1st century BCE.*

Stringhopper Biryani / Idiyappam Biryani

(30 minutes, serves 6)

This is a traditional Sri Lankan breakfast, and would be a lovely brunch option for guests. It looks a lot like fried rice, but has a notably lighter feel and flavor, and is full of healthy fresh veggies. Idiyappam biryani is gluten-free, and can easily be made vegan by skipping the egg; in that case, I might add some canned chickpeas with the potatoes, to up the protein count. Another common option is to dice 1-2 pieces of chicken and add them at the same stage.

Use whatever vegetables you have on hand—I happened to have fresh broccoli and frozen peas and corn, but carrots and chopped tomatoes are also very common, and add some nice color to the dish. Garnish with cashews and sultanas sautéed briefly in ghee for a slightly fancier presentation; you can also save the chopped omelette to use as garnish, rather than mixing it in.

This freezes well, so you can make a big batch and then save it to bring out for unexpected guests; just reheat with a sprinkling of water in the microwave. If you happen to have frozen idiyappam available in your grocery store, it works well thawed in this recipe.

1 onion, chopped fine
¼ cup ghee or vegetable oil
1 Tbsp. ginger, minced
3 cloves garlic, minced
1 serrano chili or 3 green chilies, chopped
1 tsp. cumin seed
1 tsp. black mustard seed
1 stalk curry leaves
1 tsp. ground turmeric
1 tsp. salt
1 potato, peeled and diced small
1 cup broccoli, chopped small
½ cup frozen peas
½ cup frozen corn
¼ cup chopped cilantro
1 tsp. lime juice
2 eggs
¼ cup coconut milk
12 idiyappam
cashews and sultanas cooked in ghee, optional

1. Sauté onions in ghee on medium-high with ginger, garlic, chilies, cumin seed, black mustard seed, and curry leaves for a few minutes, stirring, until onions are partially cooked.

2. Add turmeric, salt, and potato and keep cooking, stirring as needed to prevent sticking, until potatoes are mostly cooked, five to ten minutes.

3. Add broccoli, peas, corn, coriander, and lime; keep stirring until thoroughly cooked, about five more minutes.

4. In a separate small frying pan, heat a little oil and make a two-egg omelette; remove to a cutting board and slice into strips. Add gently to vegetable mixture (or reserve for garnish).

5. Finally, add coconut milk and mix to combine, then add in idiyappam and stir gently, trying not to break up the strands too much. Serve hot with pol sambol and/or yogurt.

DRINKS

Chai

Cocktails

Falooda

Mango Lassi

Mango-Passionfruit Punch or Mimosa

Fresh Sweet Lime Juice / Thesikkai Saaru

Chai

(15 minutes, serves 4)

I've been delighted to see coffee shops across America start serving chai; as someone who for most of her adult life rarely drank coffee, it was lovely having other options. (I've recently become a coffee convert, mostly by necessity!) But I admit to often being disappointed in American coffeeshop chai—it's often made from powder, and is painfully grainy. And even when it's smooth, it's generally under-spiced and over-sweetened.

This is chai the way I like to make it when I'm feeling indulgent with myself; I vary the spices, and might also add peppercorns or nutmeg. Though I admit, most of the time at home, I just use Stash's ready-made Chai Tea bags, which are surprisingly tasty. I often have a cup of the decaf version at night, as I'm getting ready to go to bed, and then I sleep like a baby.

> 4 cups milk
> 6 black Ceylon tea bags
> 2 2-inch cinnamon sticks
> 5 cloves
> 5 cardamom pods
> 5 slices fresh ginger
> jaggery, brown sugar, or honey to taste, about 2-4 tsp.

1. In a saucepan, bring milk almost to a boil (but not quite).

2. Turn down heat and add tea, cinnamon, cloves, cardamom, and ginger. Simmer tea and spices in milk until well-brewed. The mixture should be aromatic and have a light-brown color.

3. Add sweetener to taste; stir until well blended.

4. Strain mixture through a fine sieve into four mugs. Serve hot.

Cocktails

Coconut arrack is the classic Sri Lankan hard liquor, made from the nectar of coconut flowers (not to be confused with the Middle Eastern arak, which is anise flavored, or the Indonesian arak, made from sugarcane). Traditional arrack is quite harsh, but recently more mellow versions have emerged, such as Mesh & Bone's Arakku, which is aged in halmilla (or Trincomalee maram) wood barrels. The flavor is somewhere between whiskey and bourbon.

I'm not a mixologist, so I have no precise amounts for you here—I tend to make cocktails more by feel. But these flavors go very well together, and you can adjust quantities to your taste. I'd recommend starting with about 1 ½ - 2 oz. of arrack per serving, and go from there.

＊

Arrack Sour

arrack
ginger beer
fresh lime

Combine arrack and ginger beer in a highball glass filled with ice, add the juice of a lime, and garnish with a slice of lime.

＊

Ceylon Sunrise

arrack
passionfruit cordial
lime juice
crushed lemongrass
ginger beer

Combine arrack, cordial, lime juice, and lemongrass in a cocktail glass, top up with ginger beer, and serve garnished with lemongrass.

———◆———

Planter's Tea

jaggery
hot black Ceylon tea
arrack
lime juice
cinnamon stick

Combine jaggery, hot tea, arrack, and lime juice in a punch glass, with a cinnamon stick to mix. Lovely for a holiday party, or if you're fighting a cold, or just to relax with in the late afternoon.

———◆———

Serendib

arrack
jaggery
mango puree
fresh ginger, bruised
slices of mango
lime juice
ginger beer
mint leaves

Combine ingredients in a cocktail shaker, muddle well, and pour into large glass.

Falooda

(20 minutes, serves 4)

If you like boba tea, you should definitely try falooda. One of my mother's favorites, quite ridiculously pretty, and very cooling on a hot day.

agar-agar jelly, or gelatin, diced (see below)
3 cups white sugar
2 cups water
20 drops rose essence
1-2 tsp. liquid red food coloring
ice cold milk as required, about 1 cup for each serving
crushed ice
wheat vermicelli (cooked 1" pieces), sago, or tapioca pearls (optional)
soaked tulsi or chia seeds (optional)
vanilla ice cream, crushed pistachios or cashews, sultanas (optional)

Jelly:

3 cups water
4 rounded tsp. agar-agar powder or 1 cup soaked agar-agar strands
6 Tbsp. sugar
12 drops rose essence
1 tsp. liquid red food coloring
1 tsp. liquid green food coloring

1. Make syrup: Put sugar and water in a saucepan and cook over gentle heat until sugar dissolves. Cool. Add 20 drops rose essence and 1 teaspoon red coloring. You have now made rose syrup. Set aside.

2. Make lime and/or strawberry gelatin in a large shallow dish, according to package instructions, or make rose jelly with unflavored gelatin or with agar-agar (which is vegetarian).

If using agar-agar, measure water into a saucepan and sprinkle agar-agar powder over. If agar-agar strands are used, soak at least 2 hours in cold water, then drain and measure 1 cup loosely packed. Bring to a boil and simmer gently, stirring, until agar-agar dissolves. Powder takes about 10 minutes and the strands take longer, about 25-30 minutes. Add sugar and dissolve, remove from heat, cool slightly, and add 12 drops rose essence. Divide mixture between two large shallow dishes and color one red and the other green. Leave to set.

3. When jelly is quite cold and firm, cut with a sharp knife first into fine strips, then across into small dice.

4. Put about 2 tablespoons each of diced jelly and rose syrup into each tall glass, add vermicelli, sago, or tapioca pearls if desired. Fill up with ice-cold milk (pouring slowly over the back of a spoon to preserve layers) and crushed ice. Float some soaked tulsi or chia seeds on top if desired. Other toppings might include a quenelle of vanilla ice cream, and/or some crushed pistachios or cashews, and/or some dried fruit, such as sultanas.

Mango Lassi

(10 minutes, serves 4)

Some people like their mango lassi very sweet; some like it hardly sweetened at all. It seems like that decision is best left up to the individual cook.

> several ice cubes
> 1 cup yogurt (more if desired)
> 1 jar (or 1 30 oz. can) fresh mango pieces or mango puree
> a drop or two of rose essence (careful not to add too much!)
> 3-5 cups iced water
> ¼ cup or more (or less) honey
> chopped fruit as topping

1. Crush ice in blender.

2. Add yogurt, mango, and rose essence, and blend.

3. Add 3 cups water and blend—stop blender and taste, add more water if desired until preferred consistency is reached.

4. Add honey to taste and blend; top with fruit and serve

Mango-Passionfruit Punch or Mimosa

(10 minutes, serves 4)

For most parties, I'll make either the alcoholic or the non-alcoholic version of this. I'm afraid I never measure, so add ingredients to your taste! You can garnish with slices of lime if you're feeling fancy.

> mango juice
> passionfruit juice
> ginger ale or prosecco / champagne

Combine and enjoy!

Fresh Sweet Lime Juice /
Thesikkai Saaru

(5 minutes, serves 2)

This refreshing drink is often served to guests on arrival, as they step out of the hot sun into the cool shelter of the home.

4 limes
2 cups water
½ - 1 tsp. salt
2-4 tsp. sugar (to taste)

Squeeze juice from limes, add water, salt, and sugar. Serve cold.

SWEETS

Love Cake

Mango Fluff

Marshmallows

Milk Toffee / Pal Tofi

Rich Cake

Spiced Coconut Custard / Vattalappam

Sweet Thosai / Inippu Thosai

Tropical Fruit Salad with Ginger-Lime-Honey Dressing

Tropical Fruit with Chili, Salt, and Lime

Love Cake

(2 hours, including baking time; serves dozens)

Some say this Portuguese-derived cake is called *love cake* because people made it to impress potential mates, while others say it's because of the labor of love involved in all the cutting, chopping, and grinding of the fruits, nuts, and spices (much easier these days with access to a food processor). But regardless, it tastes like love: sweet, tangy, and fragrant. My mother says it doesn't taste right without the crystallized pumpkin, which you can find at Indian grocery stores, though honestly, I like it just as well with the candied ginger. A perfect accompaniment to a cup of tea.

8 ounces butter, softened, plus more for greasing
16 ounces raw unsalted cashews
10 ounces fine granulated sugar
10 egg yolks
zest of 2 limes
zest of 1 orange
juice of 2 limes, (about 2-3 Tbsp.)
1 tsp. ground cinnamon
½ tsp. ground cardamom
¼ tsp. ground cloves
¼ tsp. ground nutmeg
½ cup honey
3 drops rose water extract (or 2 tsp. rose water)

1 tsp. vanilla extract
12 oz. semolina, toasted
3 oz. candied ginger and/or crystallized pumpkin,
  minced as finely as possible
5 egg whites
confectioners sugar for dusting (optional)

1. Preheat the oven to 250°. Grease a 9x13 baking dish with butter and line it with two layers of parchment paper. Grease the paper with butter.

2. In a food processor, grind cashews to coarse meal.

3. In a standing mixer (paddle attachment), beat 8 oz. butter and granulated sugar until creamy.

4. Add egg yolks and mix well. Add zest, juice, spices, honey, rose water, and vanilla; mix well.

5. Add semolina and mix well; add cashews and candied ginger / pumpkin and mix well.

6. In a separate bowl, beat egg whites until stiff; fold gently into cake mixture.

7. Spoon batter into prepared pan; bake for 1 hour 15 minutes, until firm to the touch. (Alternatively, spoon into buttered mini tea cake molds and bake for about 40 minutes.)

8. Let cool completely in the pan, dust with confectioner's sugar (optional), cut into squares and serve.

Mango Fluff

(15 minutes cooking time, plus time to set, serves 8)

Mango fluff was a popular dessert for kids at Sri Lankan parties when I was little, and is tremendously easy and quick to make; my kids love it. It also helps satisfy my mango craving when there are no ripe mangoes to be had for love or money. There are lots of variations on it, some with real cream instead of Cool Whip, some without gelatin, some with eggs, some with flavored gelatin, some with diced tinned fruit added in. Pineapple fluff is a popular variation in Sri Lanka. I encourage you to make it your own.

> 30 oz. can mango pulp
> 8 oz. cream cheese (room temperature, or will curdle!)
> 14 oz. can sweetened condensed milk
> 2 envelopes of gelatin (plain)
> ½ cup water
> 8 oz. Cool Whip

1   Beat cream cheese and 1 can sweetened condensed milk in a stand mixer with the paddle attachment, on high. When it's all clear, with no white pieces, then add the mango pulp, and mix.

2. While it's mixing, empty two gelatin packets into a microwave safe container with the half cup of water and soak the gelatin, stirring gently until wet through,

then microwave it for thirty seconds. Pour liquid gelatin into the mango mixture, and mix a few minutes more to combine.

3. Fold in the Cool Whip gently, transfer to a serving dish (or a set of dessert glasses for a pretty dinner party presentation), and refrigerate until set (at least four hours or overnight). Can be made a few days in advance.

Marshmallows

(45 minutes + cooling time, serves dozens)

Homemade marshmallows are so much better than store-bought—there's just no comparison. Store-bought is tasty enough for dunking in hot chocolate or toasting over a fire, but these, I happily devour, straight up. This is based on Alton Brown's recipe, which is pretty identical to traditional Sri Lankan marshmallow recipes, and probably marshmallow recipes the world over, but his offers slightly more precision. We traditionally make these at Christmas, and often color the marshmallows for extra festivity.

It is much easier to make this recipe with a candy thermometer, or with some practice making candies and knowing how to test for soft-ball stage.

3 packages unflavored gelatin
1 cup water, divided
1 ½ cups granulated sugar
1 cup light corn syrup
¼ tsp. salt
1 tsp. vanilla extract (or ⅛ tsp. rose extract)
baker's sugar (or confectioner's sugar)
nonstick spray (but not the butter kind, as it will be noticeably yellow)
pink or green food coloring (optional)

1. Butter a large 9x12 pan and dust with superfine sugar. (You can use confectioner's / powdered sugar, but the superfine adds a pleasant subtle texture

to the marshmallows. My mother would pulse granulated sugar in the food processor, so it was even less fine, and in some ways, I like that even better, with a little more crisp mouthfeel on the initial bite.) Also prepare an oiled spatula for later.

2. Empty gelatin packets into bowl of stand mixer (whisk attachment), with ½ cup water.

3. In a small saucepan (a bigger one will be heavy and hard to hold steadily at a later stage) combine the remaining ½ cup water, granulated sugar, corn syrup, and salt. Cover and cook over medium high heat for 4 minutes. Uncover and cook until the mixture reaches soft-ball stage (235° if you have a candy thermometer), approximately 8 minutes. Once the mixture reaches this temperature, immediately remove from heat; if it continues, it will swiftly turn into hard candy.

4. Turn mixer on low speed and, while running, slowly pour the sugar syrup down the side of the bowl into the gelatin mixture. (Be very careful with the sugar syrup, as it is scaldingly hot and will burn you badly if it gets on your skin.) Once you've added all of the syrup, increase the speed to high.

5. Continue to whip until the mixture becomes very thick and is lukewarm, approximately 12 minutes. Add food coloring, if using for the whole batch, during this stage. Add vanilla (or rose) during the last minute of whipping. (If adding rose extract, be careful—it's very strongly flavored, and too much will ruin the sweets. Err on the side of caution.)

6. Pour the mixture into the prepared pan, spreading it evenly (and swiftly) with an oiled spatula. (For bicolored marshmallows, pour the white half first, spread quickly, then add color and re-whip the other half, then pour over the white, spreading as needed. It won't be perfectly even, but that's fine.)

7. Dust the top with enough of the remaining superfine sugar to lightly cover. Reserve the rest for later. Allow the marshmallows to sit uncovered for at least 4 hours and up to overnight.

8. Turn the marshmallows out onto a cutting board and cut into diamond shapes (traditional). As you're cutting, lightly dust all sides of each marshmallow with the remaining superfine sugar, using additional if necessary. May be stored in an airtight container for up to 3 weeks, or frozen.

Milk Toffee / Pal Tofi

(30 minutes + cooling time, serves dozens)

This is a classic Sri Lankan dessert, but I learned this particular recipe from my aunt Marina, who learned it from her sister, Neiliya. All my aunts are brilliant cooks!. It's one of my favorites, very sweet, with a great crystalline texture that melts in your mouth (a little reminiscent of maple candy in that regard). I've re-made it several times now, with a candy thermometer, trying to pin down exact measurements. The dessert is remarkably similar to New Orleans pralines (cashews instead of roasted pecans, and cut into pieces, rather than dropped on wax paper), and I wouldn't be surprised if the Portuguese brought the dessert to both regions.

> 2 cans sweetened condensed milk
> 1 ½ lbs. sugar
> ½ can water
> ½ lb. to ¾ lb. chopped cashews (it's fine if they're roasted / salted)
> 2 Tbsp. vanilla extract
> 1 stick butter

1. Put sugar, water, and condensed milk together on medium-high in big nonstick pot, stirring briefly to combine. (It doesn't have to be nonstick, but it will be easier to clean afterwards.) Watch carefully, without stirring. While mixture is cooking, grease a 9x12 glass baking dish or cake pan with butter; also prepare an oiled spatula for later.

2. When the mixture starts boiling over (around 225° on a candy thermometer), lower heat to medium. Cook for about 10 minutes (no need to stir at this point). When it starts to thicken (watery thickness), add cashews and stir. When it thickens a bit more, add vanilla and stir (it will fizz up a bit at this). Stir slowly and constantly from this point forward.

3. When it starts sticking to the pan / pulling away from the sides (soft-ball stage, 235°), add 1 stick of butter and mix it in. As soon as the butter melts, take pot off stove and pour immediately into buttered pan, using an oiled spatula to get it all out. It should smooth out on its own. (Be careful pouring, as candy syrup will burn you badly!)

4. It will still be too soft to cut. Let cool for at least 30 minutes, then try cutting it with an oiled knife. If it doesn't stick to your knife, you can cut it into pieces; small squares are traditional. Enjoy!

Rich Cake
(Wedding/Christmas Cake)

(30-60 minutes chopping time + 2 ¼ hr baking time
+ cooling time, serves dozens)

Americans are often scared of fruitcake. There's a massive cultural myth that fruitcake is some horrid dry thing that gets pressed upon you by similarly dried-up aunts. But a real fruitcake, the kind that's related to a traditional British steamed figgy pudding, is dense, rich, moist, fruity, and pleasantly alcoholic.

The chopping is labor-intensive (and would gum up a food processor), so I'd recommend having a few friends over to help and rewarding them with slabs of fruitcake to take home. (Note the long baking time, though!) Traditionally, you would use glacé cherries and other candied fruit, but Kevin doesn't like them, so we stick to just dried fruit in ours.

2 ½ lbs. mixed dried fruit (not pineapple)
8 oz. candied ginger (if you like it—if not, just use more dried fruit)
1 lb. jam (I use a mix of whatever's in the fridge)
2-4 oz. mixed peel (optional)
8 oz. raw cashews (or blanched almonds)
¼ cup brandy (with more for pouring later)
12 oz. salted butter
1 lb. powdered sugar
12 egg yolks

2 tsp. lemon zest
½ tsp. ground cardamom
1 tsp. ground cinnamon
1 tsp. grated nutmeg
¾ tsp. ground cloves
2 Tbsp. vanilla extract
1 Tbsp. almond extract
2 tsp. rose extract
1 Tbsp. honey
8 oz. fine semolina
6 egg whites
almond paste (optional)

1. Butter and flour a 9x12 cake pan.

2. Chop dried fruit, mixed peel, and nuts finely. Combine fruits, nuts, and jam in large bowl, sprinkle with brandy, stir, cover, and leave while mixing cake. This can be done the day before, allowing the fruit more time to soak in the brandy.

3. Preheat oven to 275°. In the biggest bowl you have, cream butter and sugar until light. Add egg yolks one at a time, beating well. Add grated rind, spices, flavorings, and honey and mix well. Add semolina and beat until well combined, then mix in fruit (easiest done with your clean hand).

4. Whip egg whites until stiff and, using a wooden spoon, gently fold (as best you can) through thick, stiff mixture. Turn into prepared cake pan and bake for 2 ¼ hours—cover the cake with paper after the first hour to prevent over-browning.

5. Cool completely, preferably overnight, then remove paper and wrap cake in plastic wrap; if you like, you can sprinkle a few more tablespoons of brandy over the cold cake before wrapping it. Chill in refrigerator (or other cool place) for at least a month. Every week or so, you can unwrap it, add more brandy, and rewrap it, if you like that sort of thing.

6. Alternatively, ice the cake with almond paste and then cut the cake into small rectangles (about two fingers wide) and wrap each individually in wax paper and colored foil—this is the presentation we would use for weddings, where little girls would carry baskets of the cake around at the end of the wedding and give a little cake to each guest to take home.

Note: This cake can be kept in an airtight tin for a year or longer. It just gets better and better—I recommend making it no later than mid-November if you want to serve it at Christmas.

Spiced Coconut Custard /
Vattalappam

(90 minutes, serves 8)

This is essentially a cross between coconut milk flan + chai-style spicing, legacy of Portuguese colonialization of my little island. Using jaggery and treacle would give a darker color, more characteristic of vattalappam; you can add a little dark molasses to approximate that color and add a tasty, slightly bitter, note.

Note: When cooking for a big party, I usually double the recipe and cook it in a single large baking dish, serving it alongside a big dish of mango fluff, marshmallows, milk toffee, etc.

4 fresh eggs
½ cup jaggery (or firmly packed dark brown sugar)
½ cup maple syrup, kithul treacle, or a combination
½ cup water
1 ½ cup coconut milk
¾ cup evaporated milk
½ rounded tsp. ground cardamom
¼ rounded tsp. ground mace
pinch ground cloves
1 Tbsp. rose water

1. Preheat oven to 325°.

2. Beat eggs slightly (not 'til frothy). Dissolve jaggery in water over a low heat and then cool slightly. Add sugar syrup and maple syrup to beaten eggs, add the coconut milk, and stir to dissolve sugar.

3. Strain through a fine strainer into a large jug, add evaporated milk, spices, and rose water. Pour into individual 4 oz. custard cups. Put custard cups in a baking dish or roasting pan; put dish in the oven and carefully add water to come halfway up sides of cups. Bake until set, approximately 1 ¼ hours.

4. Cool and chill custards before serving.

Note: Old eggs have less egg volume than fresh ones, and may not set properly; if you only have old eggs, try adding an extra egg or two.

Sweet Thosai / Inippu Thosai

(30 minutes + 3 hours, serves 16)

Coconut, jaggery, and brown sugar are mixed together to make a sweet filling for this crepe-like pancake. Traditionally it would have been made with rice flour; but now wheat flour is often used, which gives a softer result. You could also try a half and half mix of rice flour and wheat flour.

> 3 ½ cup all-purpose flour
> 1 tsp. baking powder
> 1 egg
> ¼ tsp. salt
> water as needed (about 2 ½ cup)
> 2 cup fresh grated (or reconstituted desiccated) coconut
> ½ cup grated jaggery
> ½ cup brown sugar

1. Mix first five ingredients, using enough water to make a thick pancake batter.

   Note: Traditionally, you would set the batter aside for three hours at this point, but if you proceed directly to step 2, you'll still get a good result.

2. In a separate bowl, combine grated coconut, jaggery, and brown sugar; using your clean hand will allow you break up any lumps of jaggery or sugar and mix them thoroughly.

3. Stir batter again, and add a little more water to make a thinner, pourable batter.

4. Heat a small frying pan on high, grease lightly. Pour a little mixture into the pan (about ½ cup) and smooth into a circle; cook for a few minutes, until the bottom turns light golden. You can flip if you want, but there is generally no need.

5. Remove to a plate and place about a teaspoon of coconut mixture in a line down the center. (You can start the next thosai cooking at this point, so that you're alternating making thosai and filling them for maximum efficiency—or, you can make all the thosai first, covering them with  a kitchen towel to keep them warm, and then fill them.) Roll the thosai relatively tightly to make a small, neat roll. Serve warm—a lovely tiffin snack for children, or with your afternoon tea.

Note: These thosai are also yummy wrapped around a little eggplant sambol, for a savory option. A nice little party appetizer.

Tropical Fruit Salad with Ginger-Lime-Honey Dressing

The key component of this salad is the ripe avocado—not a typical fruit salad component in America, but I assure you, delicious. I first had it at the Pinnawela Elephant Orphanage, where visitors meet and feed milk to little baby elephants. I ate it at a restaurant that overlooked the river where the elephants came to bathe, and the ladies all held black parasols above their heads, to protect their complexion from the sun's rays.

This fruit salad is yummy straight up, or served over vanilla ice cream. Fruits used may include mango, papaya, starfruit, lychee, rambutan, jackfruit, passionfruit, pineapple, banana, and more...

> 1 lime
> 2 Tbsp. honey
> 2 Tbsp. fresh ginger, minced
> 4 cups fruit for salad
> 1 avocado

1. For dressing, combine the first three ingredients in a small saucepan and simmer ten minutes or so, covered. Let cool. Can be made in advance and refrigerated.

2. Cut up desired fruit (if using jackfruit, you may want to oil hands first) and mix with dressing. Serve and enjoy!

Tropical Fruit with Chili, Salt, and Lime

An alternate fruit salad, for those who like a little more kick. This is my absolute favorite, made with perfectly ripe mango, and is ideal to enjoy on the beach, graced by sun and waves. A little taste of island life.

Cut up fruit (see previous for suggestions) and season with salt, cayenne, and fresh lime juice, to taste. I like about ¼ teaspoon chili, ¼ teaspoon salt, and ½ lime for 1 cup fruit. Serves lots.

After-Dinner Digestive

A little bowl of fennel or anise seeds and rock sugar makes a lovely finish to the meal. Your guests can just spoon themselves a little bit into their palms and pop it directly in their mouths. There are brightly-colored candy-coated versions available in South Asian grocery stores and online.

ACKNOWLEDGEMENTS

his book is deeply indebted to all my readers, on Facebook and elsewhere, who offered advice, encouragement, test cooking, and demands for more recipes. It wouldn't exist without you—thank you more than I can say. Kickstarter supporters—in the challenging world of modern publishing, you made this book possible!

Thanks to my designer Jeremy John Parker, to contributing photographers Paul Goyette and Suchetha Wijenayake, and to illustrator Pamudu Tennakoon, for making this book beautiful, bringing all my words to gorgeous life. Suchetha—thank you so much for being my generous guide to Sri Lanka whenever I visit; you helped me find my way home again, and helped introduce my daughter to her homeland. We'll always remember that visit to Mt. Lavinia beach, and of course, your delicious jerky—Sri Lankans, check out Fat Guy BBQ! American barbecue, Sri Lankan style.

Appreciation as well to friends and family who have been eating my food for decades, not hesitating to offer constructive criticism along with the compliments. This is good, but maybe a little more lime juice next time? You made these dishes better. Special thanks to Aaron Lav, who answered food science questions, and to Kat Tanaka Okopnik and my sweetie, Jed Hartman, who have given exceptional feedback over the years. The best feedback, of course, is watching them clean their plates and come back for seconds.

Jed has also supported me and this project in a myriad of ways, including helping me and Kavi get to Sri Lanka in December 2018; the trip wouldn't have been possible without him, and the book would have been the poorer for it. You make everything better, sweetie.

Cultural cooking gratitude to my Sri Lankan friends and relatives who answered questions from their own memories and experience cooking—my sisters, Mirna and Sharmila Mohanraj, and friends Samanthi Hewakapuge, Suchetha Wijenayake, Sugi Ganeshananthan, Mythri Jegathesan, Rozanne Arulanandam, Elaine and Angeline Martyn, and all the rest. Talented cooks all. (Any remaining culture errors are my own.)

Most of all, to Roshani Anandappa, most excellent of friends, who has shared meals and ardent cooking discussions (not quite arguments!) with me for decades now. Someday, I swear, we'll open that Chicagoland Sri Lankan restaurant, or at least host some pop-up dinners. It's going to be fun!

Thanks as well to my aunties, exceptional cooks, all. For all the times you insisted on my taking away another stuffed-full bag of rolls and patties as I headed to the airport, I'm grateful. You'll never know how much pleasure they brought.

Anand and me.

Deep gratitude to my parents—to my mother, Jacintha Mohanraj, for her incredible cooking, of course, but also to my father, Navaratnasingam Mohanraj, who was always ready to provide a mini-lecture on Sri Lankan Tamil culture and the beauty of our language. It can be challenging for any immigrant, maintaining a connection to homeland culture in the diaspora, but my parents always did their best to help us stay connected. I'm planning to take another stab at Tamil classes someday soon.

Thanks to Kavi and Anand for falling in love with ginger-garlic chicken. You gave me hope, and every day, you give me joy.

Finally, I must thank Kevin, for all the reasons, but mostly for the many days and nights when he cooked separate meals for the children, because they were suspicious of Amma's spicy food, especially once she'd started experimenting. Often they'd taste it, but teaching them to love the vast range of Sri Lankan dishes is an ongoing process. It's getting better as they get older, but in the meantime, it's a good thing Daddy can cook.

Best of men, best of husbands.

Kevin and me, in our Oak Park kitchen, getting ready to serve friends and family a Sri Lankan New Year feast.

MARY ANNE MOHANRAJ is author of *Bodies in Motion* (Harper Collins) and fourteen other titles. *Bodies in Motion* was a finalist for the Asian American Book Awards, a *USA Today* Notable Book, and has been translated into six languages. She's received a Locus Award, a CFW Breaking Barriers Award, an Illinois Arts Council Fellowship, and more.

Mohanraj is Clinical Associate Professor of fiction and literature at the University of Illinois at Chicago, serves as Executive Director of DesiLit (DESILIT.ORG), and directs the Kriti Festival of Art and Literature (KRITIFESTIVAL.ORG). She founded and served for ten issues as editor-in-chief of *Jaggery*, a South Asian literary journal (JAGGERYLIT. COM). She serves on the board of her local garden club—she loves incorporating garden harvests into her recipes—and was recently elected to the Oak Park library board.

Mohanraj was born in Sri Lanka in 1971, and moved to America at the age of two. When she was young, her family would go back often to visit grandparents and other relatives, until the war intervened. Since the conflict ended, Mohanraj has started travelling back to Sri Lanka more often for research and pleasure. She's currently working on a video game, Sigiriya, based on 5th century Sri Lanka, in partnership with the company, Rad Magpie, and is developing a food tour and writing retreat to be held on the island.

When she's not cooking, Mohanraj is writing science fiction and superhero stories; recent books include *The Stars Change* (Sri Lankans in space), and stories for George R.R. Martin's *Wild Cards* anthology series, which is coming to Hulu soon. She lives in a creaky old Victorian in Oak Park, just outside Chicago, with her partner, Kevin, two small children, a sweet dog, and two rescued space kittens.

WWW.SERENDIBKITCHEN.COM | WWW.MARYANNEMOHANRAJ.COM

மீண்டும் சந்திப்போம்

meendum santhipom
we'll meet again

ILLUSTRATOR BIOGRAPHY

PAMUDU TENNAKOON, born and praised in Sri Lanka, is currently a first-year Ph.D student in History of Art and Architecture at Brown University. Prior to commencing her studies at Brown University, Pamudu received her B.A from Bryn Mawr College, where she majored in Growth and Structure of Cities and Fine Arts (Sculpture), and her MPhil from the School of Architecture at the University of Queensland. Her academic work focuses on colonial architecture, particularly the contemporary understandings and usages of colonial architecture. Her artistic works, on the other hand, questions the line between natural and man-made. Inspired by her previous work with wire, she is currently exploring the language of three dimensional wire drawing within two dimensional line drawing.

INDEX